THE
SAVAGE
PATH

A MEMOIR OF MODERN MASCULINITY

THE
SAVAGE
PATH

DAVID SAVAGE

KATY, TEXAS

The Savage Path: A Memoir of Modern Masculinity

ISBN (Kindle): 978-1-7362912-0-7

ISBN (Print): 978-1-7362912-1-4

Library of Congress Control Number (LCCN): 2021900361

Cover Photo by: Adam White

Edited by: Wendy K. Walters | www.wendykwalters.com

Prepared for Publication by: www.palmtreeproductions.com

Note: To respect and protect the privacy of individuals, some names and identifying details have been altered.

To contact the author, visit

www.thesavagepath.com

Men are overwhelmingly driven by the calls we feel on our lives; calls with the power of life and death; calls that build marriages, families, and societies; calls that destroy them. The noblest of all masculine journeys is to navigate a life-giving path forward through these unceasing and often contradictory calls. To succeed, we must have the winnowed wisdom of beacons like *The Savage Path* to guide us through because no man figures out noble manhood on his own. David shares this wisdom and his life with us, one good story at a time in a way that makes for very enjoyable reading.

RUSSELL RAINEY
Executive Director, Adventures For Life
www.adventures.life

What is healthy masculinity? Suggestions can be found in all the wrong places. Answers are found through life's experiences and grounding in the right stuff. David provides a candid glimpse into his life's experiences and the school of hard knocks to which every man can relate. Whether you are just starting the journey called manhood or looking for course corrections, insight will be gleaned through reading *The Savage Path*.

RICK WERTZ
President/Founder, Faithful Fathering Initiative in Texas, Inc.
www.FaithfulFathering.org

A thoroughly enjoyable read that encouraged me to reflect on my own life experiences and the value of helping others along the way.

STEVEN HEROLD
Good friend and fellow servant in the Kingdom of God

In a time when young men are likely to grow up fatherless, desperate for direction, recognition, wisdom, and love, *The Savage Path* challenges men to step up by taking the reader on a journey of hilarious life experiences and powerful principles of authentic manhood.

CHAD HEROLD
Young Adult Pastor, Second Baptist Church
Houston, Texas

David's collection of highly entertaining, true-life adventures presents powerful life lessons learned through embracing positive masculinity on the journey to manhood. A timely read for young men or parents and grandparents (like me) that illustrates, through clever storytelling, solid direction on how to promote and grow traditional, cornerstone Christian values for men of all ages. Presented in a no-nonsense, practical manner, *The Savage Path* is a wonderful blueprint of sorts that views masculinity as a God-given positive designation and embraces this view through captivating stories as one boy grows into manhood.

MARY NALEPKA SMITH
Childhood friend

I am drawn to authenticity. And raw honesty. I especially like real-life help mixed with real-life hope for being a better man. And in the stir of David Savage's life story, you powerfully get all three. From his "whole life perspective," you not only travel with him through his life, but you also feel he is mentoring you in the best of manhood along the way. These are "not to be missed" insights from which any man—but especially younger men—can greatly benefit. Men today don't need fluff. They need THE TRUTH. They don't need easy. They need *THE SAVAGE PATH*! I promise you, a wealth of truth is exposed through David's story of successes and failures. That's why I highly recommend it!

DR. ROBERT LEWIS
Author, Founder of Men's Fraternity / BetterMan
www.betterman.com

A good woman desires a good man. We want strong, caring, character-filled men to fulfill the roles of father, husband, brother, son, and friend. The culture war has confused the definitions of manhood and masculinity and blurred the lines between what is healthy and what is toxic, and has replaced what is morally responsible with what is socially acceptable. David Savage clears the fog and sends out a clear signal beacon for today's man—a clarion call for authentic masculinity that challenges men to reach for the best version of themselves and take their place in society unapologetically. I found this book refreshing and a delight. I want all the men in my life that I care about to experience David's journey and be encouraged to walk out their own.

WENDY K. WALTERS
Author, Editor, Coach, Motivational Speaker
www.wendykwalters.com

BUT AS FOR YOU, O MAN
OF GOD, FLEE EVIL. PURSUE
RIGHTEOUSNESS, GODLINESS,
FAITH, LOVE, STEADFASTNESS,
GENTLENESS.

PAUL, THE APOSTLE

DEDICATION

This book is dedicated to the four sons God has entrusted to me and who will father the next generation of our family one day to give me the joy of being a grandfather.

Dayton Savage—son

Geoffrey McClard—stepson

Shaun McClard—stepson

William Seldon—son-in-law

ACKNOWLEDGEMENTS

I would like to acknowledge my father, Wilbur E. Savage Jr, my mother Minnie Savage, and my older brother, Richard Savage, who first modeled tremendous courage very early in my life. All three have since passed away but have left their imprint upon me forever.

I owe a great debt to many BSA leaders and the scouting program in general, but I would like to specifically mention my first Scoutmaster James B. Heath and Frank T. Hilton, my Camp Director and boss while on staff at summer camp. Both of these men were very influential in my formative years and instilling all the best qualities in me that the scouting program aspires to achieve.

During my college years and throughout my life, I have been supported and encouraged by the many brothers of the Alpha Tau Omega Fraternity I came to know and grow with in my young adult life. It was and remains a true brotherhood experience.

My spiritual development was greatly enhanced by all of the pastors I have been fortunate enough to know along my Savage Path, as well as the Emmaus Community and Reunion Groups. Without a doubt, the strongest influence in my life for the last eighteen years has been my current pastor and teacher, Dr. Ed Young at Second Baptist Church in Houston, Texas. It has been his illumination of God's Word that has given me the courage to step out in faith and write this book. I am extremely humbled and grateful for his foreword in endorsing this project.

The members of the "Sixpack": Adolph Lechtenberger, Jim Schepens, John Stacy, Joe Christo, and Mike Nash who I backpacked with for eighteen consecutive years from 1991 through 2009 and who remain close friends shared a great deal of their wisdom and life experience with their much more junior member. As the younger man, I have continued on our tradition with new recruits younger than me. Some were only one-timers, but those who have remained steadfast and continue to adventure with me are Clay Brown, Nigel Hilton, and Adam White. These men have helped me continue to "sharpen the saw," as Stephen Covey calls his seventh habit.

Although this book is targeted to a male audience, I have received tremendous support from the lovely women in my life. My two sisters, Kathy McBurnie and Terry Savage Gibson, have always believed in me and helped me with the facts around our childhood and other family history covered in this book. My daughter Nicole Selden has lent her considerable skills in all things social media and construction of the website to help get the word out for my book. Of course, my wife Kimberly has loved me through all of my various adventures and projects and is leading up the book launch team. I am eternally grateful to her.

Lastly, I must praise and acknowledge my editor and publishing assistant, Wendy K. Walters, who has taught me everything I know about becoming an author. She has reviewed every word and kept me out of the ditches. This entire project began with her wonderful anointing prayer in our first Zoom meeting which confirmed for me that God's hand was over this project. She has provided great energy and encouragement in addition to her considerable talents related to writing and publishing a book.

JUDGE A MAN BY HIS QUESTIONS
RATHER THAN BY HIS ANSWERS.

VOLTAIRE

THE SAVAGE PATH

CONTENTS

FOREWORD

BY DR. ED YOUNG
PASTOR, SECOND BAPTIST CHURCH, HOUSTON

Many years ago, I preached a sermon entitled, "The Rise of the Purple Penguins." I had read a newspaper report about an elementary school teacher who directed parents to refrain from identifying their incoming student as either male or female. She went on to explain that in her classroom, gender was neutral, and the children would neither be identified with color labels like pink or blue nor gender labels like male and female. Instead, they were all equal— *purple* penguins. The article disturbed me, and I reached into God's Word to refute the rise of purple penguins based on Genesis 5:2 and Mark 10:6, where we are clearly told that God created male and female.

Since that article all those years ago, the idea of purple penguins has become less absurd and more accepted in our culture. David Savage steps out with boldness on a topic that has fallen prey to our cancel-culture. He speaks with courage and truth as he embraces the importance of manhood and masculinity—cultural taboos—but biblical truths.

The book reads like a conversation with a friend. David artfully takes us on his journey with concise prose, delightful illustrations, and biblical reverence. Don't shy away from this topic. *The Savage Path* leads us away from dangerous cultural pitfalls toward a path that is savage in its pursuit of God's best.

—DR. ED YOUNG
Pastor Second Baptist Church Houston

THE QUEST FOR
AUTHENTIC MASCULINITY

Just having eclipsed my sixtieth birthday, I gazed at the hourglass on my desk. One cannot avoid thinking of the sand volume in terms of a true measurement of one's mortal life span. It is an undeniable fact that there is more sand in the bottom than there is left in the top. Such a milestone demands a big picture assessment. A few questions regarding my path come to mind for me and maybe for my reader as well.

Where am I right now?

Where did I begin?

What hard-won wisdom have I gained along the way?

Why write a book now?

What makes me qualified to write a book on the topic of positive masculinity?

Let me try to answer these questions briefly and hopefully motivate you to read the entire book.

Today, I am retired after a very successful engineering career, the first five years as a civil engineering consultant, and then a thirty-one-year career in chemical engineering technical sales and management. My title at retirement was Area Vice President Global Downstream Corporate Accounts. For the last twenty years, I have traveled extensively throughout North America and around the world as a contract negotiation expert and relationship manager for our largest clients. Since retiring, I have been appointed by the Governor of Texas to the Board of Directors of the Brazos River Authority. Personally, I have been married, divorced, remarried, and raised a blended family with four adult children today.

I am a native West Texan, born and raised primarily in San Angelo, the youngest of four children and son of an Air Force Master Sergeant. My high school years and football district were where the real "Friday Night Lights" took place in what was then referred to as the "Little Southwest Conference." We lived in a twelve hundred and twenty-four square foot, three-bedroom, one-bath very modest home. I was baptized and confirmed a Methodist but became a Baptist in 2002 and am proud to call myself a devoted Christian, serving as a Deacon since 2006 in my current Baptist Church. Through travel with my church, my wife and I visited Israel in 2008 and had the opportunity to be rededicated in baptism in the Jordan River, where Christ was baptized. We have also visited China and Normandy, France traveling with our church.

In the first quarter of 2019, after managing the affairs of my mother and older brother in separate memory care facilities for the previous five years, I lost them both—exactly six weeks apart. My father passed away in 2006 from lung cancer, and I have somehow found myself the reluctant family patriarch, although I was the baby in our family of four children.

Thanks to COVID-19, 2020 will be known as the "lost year" for most of us. Many plans for weddings, vacations, and any kind of travel have been postponed or canceled. With much more time at home due to remote working and at home schooling, we have all been given a time out to do some reevaluating. Other disturbing events of 2020 include social unrest and the polarization of our country politically. We all hate to see this and are deeply searching for answers as to how and why we got to this place. After speaking with many other people from all kinds of backgrounds, I believe one issue at the root of this is a failure of true leadership. The culture war has led our nation into a wilderness.

A wilderness is a dangerous place because it is unmapped, unknown, and uninhabited except for wild animals that can harm us. A wilderness is also an easy place to get lost, and I think the young American male is the creature most in danger. Masculinity, in any form, has been viciously attacked for decades with serious unintended consequences. Our society desperately needs genuine, healthy masculinity. We need boys to grow into responsible, productive men and fathers. We need their strength to face down evil. And they need a guide to help them navigate this new wilderness, to find and define their masculinity in

MASCULINITY, IN ANY FORM, HAS BEEN VICIOUSLY ATTACKED FOR DECADES WITH SERIOUS UNINTENDED CONSEQUENCES.

the gender-confused world of today. This is why I felt called, or more strongly, commanded to write this book.

I have been observing the ascendency of our succeeding generation and think that I just might have something they want now before taking the helm of our society, the truth. Yes, good old fashioned, unapologetic, look you straight in the eye and deliver the facts **truth**. This is why I am writing this book now.

You see, for thirty-one years, I worked for the world's largest water treatment chemical company, and one of my primary jobs, constantly, throughout that career was to break emulsions; mixtures of oil and water that will not separate into the two distinct phases we know exist. An example of an emulsion is mayonnaise, content to remain a blend somewhat stably unless heated, stressed, or aged. When it does separate, it is quite clear visually that there are two phases, which look completely different. This rising generation has been fed an emulsified blend of culture which confuses the clear separation between American exceptionalism and American shame. I became an expert in applying precise chemistry to snap those emulsions into two clear and distinct phases, almost instantly. The chemistry metaphor here is the truth. We hear much too little of it these days. What I like so much about it is that it is very simple. There is male and female in almost every species of living thing on the planet, and that includes human beings. It's not a multiple-choice test. And our society needs a big, booster dose of healthy positive, spiritual-leader-

THE RISING GENERATION HAS BEEN FED AN EMULSIFIED BLEND OF CULTURE WHICH CONFUSES THE CLEAR SEPARATION BETWEEN AMERICAN EXCEPTIONALISM AND AMERICAN SHAME.

of-the-family masculinity before it all evaporates or is boiled off to vapor!

The dictionary defines poison as a substance with an inherent property that tends to destroy life or impair health. Certain elements of our society have coined a phrase known as "toxic masculinity." This doctrine is itself a poison intended to destroy life or impair the health of our current society. The extremely popular shorthand today, PC, supposedly stands for political correctness, whatever that is. But I submit to you that its true intentions are poison and control. It demands a response and an antidote!

I will admit that my generation, the Baby Boomers, has not stewarded the country extremely well and has already put the rising generation through high divorce rates and a general absence of good role models. But just as with any endangered species (the young, physically, mentally, and morally healthy American male), we should all rally to save those required to play a pivotal role in maintaining the greatest experiment in freedom and liberty ever attempted, the one created by America's founding fathers.

This book is one humble man's memoir describing his journey through life with its successes, failures, friendships, and family. No business ever captures one hundred percent market share, and I suspect that there will be people who disagree with my views in this book as presented. But it is not my intent to offend anyone either. I have tried to use humility and humor to highlight the hard-won wisdom I have gleaned along my path. Much of what I have learned and wish to share has come from real wilderness adventures. I invite you to sit by my campfire, feel its warmth, and let it draw you into the intimate storytelling environment that only its flickering flame and the expansive night sky can provide. You are entering a sacred place where we will engage the genuine pursuit of authentic manhood. We will share tall tales, triumphs, and tragedies. And like the real wilderness, when we get lost, it is best to admit it sooner rather than later and backtrack onto the map we have with us.

I am not promising perfection, only my own true journey to grow into the kind of man who can fulfill his Maker's purpose for him: Find a work to do, a woman to love, and will to obey.

COURAGE IN CATASTROPHE

Much has changed between 1960 (when I was born) and now. Our ability to understand the challenges we face today requires that we respect history's context, thus gaining the benefit of perspective, both past and present, across the span of time. So, let's go back one hundred years prior to my birth to 1860. I was born in the Concho Valley area, where San Angelo, Texas, is today. This territory was known as Comancheria Country—Indian country—and it was totally controlled by the best light cavalry warriors in North American history, the Comanche Indians. They thought their way of life was securely under their control, but we have seen how unkind history was to the tribe whose Indian name was translated simply as "The People."

I was the youngest of four children, two boys and two girls, Air Force brats and Baby Boomers all. In order of appearance, here are the names and year born below for my immediate family:

Wilbur E. Savage Jr.	January 1932
Minerva (Minnie) Savage	September 1934
Richard Savage	November 1953
Kathleen (Kathy) Savage	April 1956
Teresa (Terry) Savage	January 1959
David Savage	September 1960

To set the stage for the early sixties and contrast it to today's cultural concerns, here are several important events in the United States shortly after I was born.

1963 family portrait of the four Savage children

In November 1962, we experienced the Cuban Missile Crisis with Russian nuclear missiles less than 100 miles from U.S. shores. President John F. Kennedy handled it well with a naval blockade, which was the closest we came to a military confrontation with Russia during the Cold War. It is safe to say that this event constituted the zenith of the Cold War.

One year later, in November of 1963, President Kennedy was assassinated, and Vice President Johnson became President of the United States.

We were an Air Force family, and my father was assigned to work in the 6910th Security Wing Headquarters in Darmstadt, Germany, in early 1964. At the time, we didn't really know what my father did. We learned much later that he was involved in the top-secret analysis of Russian signal intelligence and troop movements.

So here we were, a family of six in a foreign land at the peak of the Cold War with my dad playing a pivotal role in spying on the other side. My mother was not yet 30 years old, and everything to do with setting up and caring for the four of us kids fell to her.

We had not been in Darmstadt a full year yet when the first catastrophe struck our family. My mother clipped and saved the article written in the Air Force newspaper Stars & Stripes. It states:

SGT'S SON BADLY HURT WHEN STRUCK BY AUTO

DARMSTADT, GERMANY (S&S)—Richard Savage, 10-year-old son of S Sgt and Mrs. Wilbur E. Savage from the 6910th Security Wing here, received severe injuries when struck by a German auto while attempting to cross a main thoroughfare.

Young Savage received a compound fracture of the left leg and severe lacerations on his back and chest when he dashed in front of an auto driven by Wolfgang Mueller from Bensheim.

The accident happened on Heidelberger Strasse, adjoining the Lincoln Village housing area. The youngster was reported in good condition Monday at the 97th General Hospital in Frankfurt.

As a four-year-old, I have no recollection of when the accident occurred. I know that it shook my parents up, but they were trained to keep secrets and maintain good poker faces. Being in Germany with your family, thinking that the Russians were going to roll into West Germany at any time, must have demanded incredible courage on the part of both of my parents. It had to be devastating and terrifying to have no help from family with four young children and the oldest, a 10-year-old, struck by a car and near fatally hurt. But my very brave parents walked the talk of the well-known British motto, "Keep Calm and Carry On." All I remember is that I was pleased to be a fetcher of anything my older brother Rick wanted or needed while he wore the cast. He was my hero and idol. Ironically, eight years later, when Rick was drafted for the Vietnam War, he failed the physical based upon the staph infection he had contracted from this terrible accident. What had nearly killed him might have truly saved his life later. Unfortunately, our family was not done with catastrophes in Darmstadt yet either.

The Savage Children after Rick's Accident 1964

My very earliest, vivid memory was the following year when I was five years old. Our family lived in a three-story apartment building in Lincoln Village, the housing area for military families mentioned in the newspaper article previously. It was the day after Christmas 1965. I was playing on the floor in our apartment with a bright orange and yellow dump truck I had gotten from Santa. My sister Terry was also on the floor, and we were discussing what cargo she could provide from her toy stash for my dump truck. After pushing the truck around a few feet on my knees, I glanced down our hallway and saw a huge rolling black cloud of smoke. I yelled, "Mommy, look, smoke!"

She immediately told all of us to head to the door to get out of the apartment. Like the selfish child I was, I instinctively ran to retrieve my prized possessions from my room, which was closest to the front room: my new toy rifle, my blanket (as a prolific thumb sucker), my cowboy hat, and "Pamby," my little stuffed panda bear and constant companion. With my booty in hand, I raced to the front door as we all exited the apartment, which was growing more and more engulfed in flames and smoke.

They say that smell is the sense most closely associated with memory, and if you have ever smelled your own house and belongings burn, you would agree vehemently. The acrid smell of burnt things and the smoke afterward may be why it is so vivid to me as my first recall. It was very cold outside with old accumulated snow all over the ground and perhaps a few inches of fresh snow. We kids

Christmas Day with my cowboy hat, rifle, and sisters as captives

were in our pajamas and were barefoot, although we had blankets around our bodies. I was so taken by the whole scene of fire trucks with sirens and lights flashing, people speaking in German about how to go about putting the fire out (I assumed), hearing them chop with axes through the flooring to get to the wiring source of ignition, and the hiss of high-pressure water flooding our apartment and gushing out area rugs to the balcony.

That all happened very quickly in my mind, and then I saw my dad coming up from work in his Air Force uniform, looking for us with great concern amongst all the lights and trucks. It was a surreal, "being in a movie" moment in which no one would ever want to be. After the fire was extinguished, we watched them throw most of our belongings off the third-floor balcony to create a pile of debris on top of the old snow. It was a catastrophic event for our family, and I remember my mother sifting through the rubbish heap for pieces of treasured photo albums that might be salvageable.

Those first five years of my life were quite a jarring string of events, and yet, I never felt extremely insecure or saw my parents behaving anything other than normal when dealing with us children. Building character is very similar to building a house; it has to have a firm, well-constructed foundation. My parents' courage and bravery through those five years provided a tremendous foundation for my siblings and me. We didn't hide and evade tough situations or unforeseen circumstances; we faced them head-on together as a family and went through the adversity, no matter what kind of catastrophe it may have been. Living in a foreign country far from our family and friends made our family unit tight. I was glad that we had, by today's standards, a large family with four children. This meant you had more playmates to share those memories with and that our parents just couldn't afford the time to dote on one particular child. Now, stop and think for a minute about families today and contrast the courage and bravery demonstrated, or perhaps absent, when facing the dangers of our time.

THRIFT LEADS TO INNOVATION

There I was, sitting at the kitchen table staring at a plate still loaded with a helping of what was now, quite cold, broccoli. This was becoming a far too common occurrence in my estimation as a nine-year-old. I loathed broccoli! The smell of it in the house when my mom began cooking it disgusted me—and it wasn't just broccoli either. I felt the same way about the smell of cauliflower and brussels sprouts. When it came to texture, mushrooms and asparagus were my nemeses. Yes, I was truly the pickiest of all picky eaters and equally stubborn in my resistance to ingesting such horrible food.

And there *they* were also! My two older sisters, Kathy and Terry— the sentinels. Our family rules were that you could not leave the table or have dessert until you ate everything served to you on your plate. I was a world-class holdout, dramatically gagging on split pea soup, pleading, negotiating, begging favors from my sisters. I can't really imagine *what* my parents thought about their youngest child's behavior, only that his will must be broken. Give no quarter!

And yet, that is exactly how this scene would typically end up playing out. Neither of my sisters wanted to spend their entire evening posted as a sentinel watching me stare silently at my plate.

I would whisper to them in desperation, "How about a quarter each to let me give it to the dogs or throw it away in my napkin?"

The deal was done, and it was worth every penny! The only problem was that we ate these vegetables far more often than I got my meager fifty cents per week allowance. On top of that, it would mean that I would be the only child who would not have movie money for the Saturday matinee at the Air Force Base movie theater we lived nearby. This situation was a real conundrum—not to mention unsustainable! This wilderness was far colder and crueler than I deserved.

Easter photo with my "vegetables face" during sentinel years with my sisters

Now, I believe God has several common purposes for every man, and finding a "work to do" is one of them. Often times, your gifts and talents are revealed quite early in life as a child. I believe this was the first clue in revealing my propensity for independent problem solving, the life purpose of every engineer. And as any engineer will tell you, the first step in solving any problem is defining that problem. Mine was quite clear. There were multiple times each week that I refused to eat the vegetables prepared for dinner. The only solution that had presented itself previously was the extortion of my allowance by my sisters. I had become quite resourceful in collecting my dad's aluminum beer cans and stomping them flat in my hiking boots to supplement my small allowance with recycling revenue. I had even roamed the neighborhood and driving range on the base, searching for empty Coke® bottles to return for the five-cent deposit. There just wasn't enough income available to me to meet my considerable bribery needs. What became crystal clear in my mind was that I needed a way to make vegetables disappear! This mission became my problem statement and the life purpose to which I would devote every ounce of spare thought and energy until I found out how to do it.

There is something very fulfilling about having a single-minded purpose to achieve something. I threw myself into the task. It didn't take long for me to find a solution. How does anyone make something disappear? With magic, of course!

I had an extensive comic book collection, and every issue had an ad on the inside front cover selling some small magic device or booklet on card tricks. I cut out cereal box proof of purchase seals, collected S&H Green Stamps, and when the opportunity presented itself, I even thieved loose change from my older brother and sisters. I knew I had to become a master magician in order to make my vegetables disappear before my family's very eyes each evening at the dinner table.

I hatched an ingenious plan! I was able to procure a large box of fireplace matches; these are much longer than regular matches, so the box was about six inches long by three inches wide. It had the classic slide-out tray that held the matches, and the outer shell, which the tray fit neatly inside, had the striker material on the sides. It was perfect! When no one else was around the house, I glued the shell under the table at the position where I always sat for our meals. I tested how smoothly the tray could slide in and out of the outer box. Then, I practiced doing it repeatedly under the table without looking until it was very natural, and almost no movement of my hands was visible above the table. The prop was in place, and I was giddy with excitement to try out my new scheme.

The mind of a magician circa 1970

Every magician knows that the key to any successful trick is in the deception or early distraction. This was a particular problem since I had the most well-established pattern of behavior known to man. Would anyone in my family actually believe that I was suddenly eating these vegetables?? Again, another early character trait was revealed—salesmanship. I had the gift of gab! My parents always wanted to hear about our day at school and what was going on in our lives. Rick was seven years my elder, so he was sixteen at the time and had just received his driver's license. He wasn't too keen on reporting out the new frontiers he was exploring. In those awkward years of adolescence, my sisters were becoming young women and were generally much quieter and reluctant to talk. Perhaps the best thing for me was that this was not something new in my behavior. As the youngest, I always sought attention somehow and typically talked a lot at dinner prior to my scheme. I simply talked to avoid eating my vegetables.

The night of my first performance came, and I was extremely jubilant to try out my solution. I immediately launched into some fascinating story about the space program we had learned at school that day. It was 1969 or early 1970, and we had just landed a man on the moon. My brother was a prolific model builder, and our room was full of his master works, including a three-foot-tall Saturn rocket. I was genuinely interested in everything related to the space program, so this was not too contrived a topic. As I talked excitedly about the astronauts, I was simultaneously flicking broccoli into the napkin on my lap and then quickly transferring it into the tray I had deftly slid out from the matchbox under the table.

In no time, I had transferred all of the material from my plate into the matchbox and secured it back in place to the box glued under the table. I kept a tiny fraction of broccoli on the plate to dramatically swirl in my mashed potatoes and announced for the whole family to observe that I had eaten my vegetables first while they were still hot! Voilà!! It truly was magic, and it had worked! I'm not sure if it was just how hard my family had hoped that one day this would happen and chose to believe what they wished for, or if it was my extensive preparation and planning, but believe it they did! I was asked to stand up. My pockets were searched. The dogs were cross-examined and inspected for traces of the dreadful vegetable. The countenance of my sisters fell as they realized their income streams had just contracted— what a moment of pure satisfaction that was! I will never forget it. You could have hung an Olympic gold medal around my neck, and I could not have been any prouder. But it had to remain a secret!

Later that evening, I went to the kitchen when no one else was around and removed the contents out of the matchbox and took it all the way to the alley where we put the trash out for collection so it would not be discovered. I knew suspicion still lurked in their hearts.

I did not know it at the time, but at the tender age of nine, I was beginning to formulate my first understanding of a supply chain. Trying to pull off magic before my family's very eyes, perhaps multiple times in a single week, was a risky proposition. I needed alternatives to be certain the stench of broccoli never neared my lips. My second bright idea was to move up the supply chain and intercept the offending vegetables the same day they came home from the grocery store. I decided to always be on hand when my mother came home from the base commissary with our groceries to help "put them away." In fact, I would try to go to the commissary with her when I could so that I could pull things like liver out of the shopping basket and hide it somewhere on the aisle we happened to be going down so that it would not even make it to the checkout. It was only when she got home and reviewed the receipt that she would realize she had somehow forgotten it. If the undesired vegetables did make it to the house, I would hide them quickly somewhere in a cabinet of pots and pans and later go back to dispose of them down the toilet or remove them to the alley trash. I knew she would catch on eventually since those items were indeed on the receipt, but I would attempt to blame the sackers who worked for tips of forgetting to bag those items.

Like most criminals, it was only a matter of time before I made a mistake. Of course, it was with a package of frozen broccoli, my cursed adversary. We had a corner cabinet with a circular lazy Susan where we kept our larger pots and pans. It was down low and easy for me to reach. I grabbed the frozen broccoli and stashed it off of the lazy Susan in the corner of the cabinet, so if it were rotated, the package wouldn't come into view. Unfortunately, an episode of *The Flintstones* or some other television show distracted me, and I forgot about it completely. A day or two later, it had thawed and was stinking horribly. My mom sniffed it out, and I knew when I heard the middle name invoked with a full crescendo, "David *Lawrence* Savage!" The jig was up.

In my feeble attempt at courtroom defense, I stated that she could not be certain it was me. There were a total of six people living in this home, and there were no witnesses. The punishment was swift and sure, as it should be in a system of true justice.

The old matchbox ruse was remarkably reliable for years until the older siblings began leaving for college or having so many evening activities that we were seldom sitting down as a family for meals anymore. The funniest thing is that I took that same kitchen table with me as I went off to Texas A&M University myself nine years later in 1978. As we flipped it over to remove the legs for moving, my mom wondered out loud about the greasy spot on the underside of the table where I had always sat. I finally confessed to my scheme, feeling that I was well past the statute of limitations. She was incredulous! I did point out that I had grown to become the tallest and strongest member of our family even as a strictly "meat and potatoes" man!

I challenge you to be a man of resourcefulness and action in the wilderness. Sitting there, staring at the plate wasn't going to make those vegetables go away. I had to think through the problem and take action. I encourage you to look for ways to avoid passivity and waiting for others to solve your problems. As you do, search for clues that point to your gifts, which will then help you find your work to do.

AVOID PASSIVITY
AT ALL COSTS.

DON'T WAIT FOR
OTHERS TO SOLVE YOUR
PROBLEMS; BE A MAN
OF RESOURCEFULNESS
AND ACTION.

THE SIGNIFICANCE OF CEREMONY

I had a wonderful scouting experience growing up in San Angelo, Texas as a member of Troop 3 sponsored by Goodfellow Air Force Base, where my father worked. Our scoutmaster was Jim Heath, Chief Master Sargeant of the Noncommissioned Officers (NCO) Academy there on the base. He was a fit, tough, crew-cut wearing, Camel cigarette smoking; you say, "sir," and "ma'am," man. Mr. Heath, as we scouts called him, took Troop 3 to Camp Sol Mayer, one of two camps operated by the Concho Valley Council of the BSA, each and every summer back in the early seventies. In 1972 I attended summer camp at Camp Sol Mayer for the first week away from my family as an eleven-year-old. One very early lesson came from Mr. Heath regarding the fifth point of the Scout Law, a scout is courteous. He was quite firm about a scout answering an adult with a "Yes, sir" or "No, sir."

I wasn't that keen on it myself, but I would soon learn why he had brought a one-pound coffee can painted yellow with a big number five in black on it. It had a baling wire handle, and any scout who did not answer with a snappy "Yes, sir" was obliged to carry the can around with him **_everywhere_** throughout the camp. I had it in the dining hall for meals, at merit badge classes, and even by my cot when I slept. He gave me chances to get rid of it, but as you learned a little about my strong will in the previous chapter, I did not avail myself of that opportunity. Instead of "yeah," I tried "okay" and other evasions of discipline like nodding my head. Each time I failed, I got a big rock put in the can and soon I was carrying a can full of rocks everywhere I went. Eventually, I yielded to Mr. Heath's authority, and one by one, got rid of each rock, and after a day or two of learning my lesson in courteousness, I finally got rid of the can itself. I did not forget the lesson!

Scoutmaster Jim Heath at the Lonesome Pine Campsite, Camp Sol Mayer

The nearest town to Camp Sol Mayer was Fort McKavett, Texas, a tiny spec of a town nearly right in the center of the state. Fort McKavett was a frontier fort established as Camp on the San Saba River in 1852 to protect settlers from Comanche raids. It was later renamed in honor of Captain Henry McKavett, who was killed in the Mexican-American War. This area of West Texas is dry and difficult, full of prickly pear cactus, rattlesnakes, and mesquite trees. Water has always been a precious and prized resource in West Texas, and the San Saba riverbanks were an oasis of flora and fauna for we young scouts to explore. The river itself was where we earned our swimming, lifesaving, rowing, and canoeing merit badges. It was along this river that I experienced my first Order of The Arrow "Tap Out Ceremony" around a blazing campfire.

I knew that we had held elections at a troop meeting back in the Spring for the few slots available to our troop for initiation into this honor society. However, since I was too young to be considered, I had forgotten about it. I had no idea about what that selection ceremony would be like or how it would be conducted at summer camp. The ceremony came late in the week after we had all become more comfortable with camp life and routines.

We were told to put on our dress uniforms and conduct ourselves very formally for this ceremony with absolutely **_no_** talking! Each troop formed a single file line from their camp and quietly marched toward a distant, slow drumbeat to a torchlit area down near the river, which we had not seen previously. The heat of

AUTHOR'S NOTE:
The Order of the Arrow, or OA as it is known in scouting circles, is the national Honor Society of the Boy Scouts of America (BSA). It is composed of scouts and scouters who best exemplify the Scout Oath and Law in their daily lives as elected by their peers. It uses imagery commonly associated with American Indian cultures for its self-invented ceremonies. These ceremonies are usually for recognition of leadership qualities, camping skills, and other scouting ideals, as exemplified by their elected peers.

the day had passed, as one of the blessings regarding the low humidity of West Texas was the rapid fall in temperatures as soon as the sun went down. I was taking it all in for the very first time, observing full and elaborate Indian costumes on the older teenage boys solemnly pounding the tom-tom. The remnants of daylight allowed for a good view of the scene as we all were placed in a very large circle around an enormous, six-foot, log-cabin-structured campfire that had yet to be lighted. The Indians who held the torches had stern expressions, staring down those who dared to make eye contact. All of them had war paint on their faces with mostly red and yellow colors. Most had only a single feather with a leather headband, but one impressive chief had a full headdress presiding near the campfire logs.

In the distance, we heard chanting or some kind of slow Indian song. It was coming from the river. As the dusk light fell, a chorus of frogs began to croak along a large shallow area of lily pads near the bank. Seemingly, in perfect unison with the approaching canoes and growing volume of the Indian chant, more and more frogs began to join the chorus in a crescendo of croaking louder than I had ever heard before. It seemed like thousands of frogs were conscripted into this special ceremony, and the hair began to rise on the back of my neck as I saw, about 100 yards up the river slowly paddling toward us, a muscular Medicine Man standing in a canoe with a paddler behind him and a torchbearer in front of him. As they approached, we could make out more of his spectacular costume. His face was fully painted blue on one half and white on the other half. He had a huge headdress with curved ram's horns on both sides of a white wool or goat hair skull cap that had red fox furs dangling down like earrings on both sides of his face. He had no shirt on, and only a breechcloth covered his lower body in front and behind. He had a blue sun with white rays painted on his chest and leather straps with bells on both biceps and calves. As the canoe slowly pulled along the bank, the other Indians rushed in to hold it steady as he stepped out onto the riverbank. He wore beaded moccasins on his feet, and in one hand, he held a huge bull snake with several coils around his forearm. In the other hand, he held a large gourd rattle. As the tom-tom pounded and the frogs sang, crickets began to chirp in behind us to add to the cacophony in the otherwise silent setting. The chanting had stopped once the Medicine Man stepped from the canoe, and I'm sure many mouths were agape as the first-timers, like me, drank in the scene. None of us knew what was going to happen next. The suspense was tremendous!

Bob Kamensky as Meteu, the Medicine Man

The tom-tom stopped the drumbeat, and we could hear the crackling of the torches around us now and smell the kerosene smoke as they moved inside the circle, making their way to the Chief standing by the still unlit stack of wood. They exchanged greetings, and then the Chief greeted all of those present in a loud, firm voice. We learned that the Chief's name was Allowat Sakima, Chief of the Fire of the Lenni Lenape tribe, and the Medicine Man's name was Meteu. For parents in attendance in the large circle, he explained the evening's significance and its purpose in selecting the "Ordeal Candidates," as they were called, to the Brotherhood of Cheerful Service. He then bowed in each direction, acknowledging nature and elements to the East, West, North, and South. Finally, the Chief of the Fire called upon the Great Spirit to be with us, and the stack of wood spontaneously exploded into flames with no one standing near it! I thought to myself, "Now, if you want to impress an eleven-year-old boy, this was the way to do it! Now, what!?"

Next, Chief Allowat Sakima stepped out of the large circle to walk behind the group while Meteu, the Medicine Man, began to dance inside the circle, bells jangling with every step, shaking his gourd rattle in a hypnotizing rhythm with the beat of the tom-tom. Meteu moved close to each participant's face with a torchbearer behind him, searching the eyes of every person in the circle. He was chanting and shaking the bull snake on his arm as he danced and proceeded around the circle. Suddenly, he jumped backward to stand before a candidate face to face, shouting loudly and scaring the daylights out of all of us!

Kitchkinet, the Guide, followed behind Meteu, carrying a long stick with an arrow necklace for each candidate. It was uncomfortable binder's twine tied on either end to a small carved arrow about six inches long. Meteu placed the necklace (which was really a bit like in a horse's mouth) around the candidate's neck and shoved the bit in the candidate's mouth to assure silence. From behind the candidate, Chief Allowat Sakima firmly placed both of his hands palm down on the candidate's shoulders. He then "tapped" with one hand on the shoulder of the candidate with his palm down three times to signify the three points of the Scout Oath while securely holding the other shoulder with his other hand. Then, changing hands, he tapped the other shoulder once with a pause, then two times closer together to represent the twelve points of the Scout Law. Another Indian character named Nutiket, the Guard, then took a huge glinting knife blade and raked it across the candidate's forehead, leaving a deep red mark, and shoved him back into the arms of two braves who quickly whisked the candidate away up a hill behind the circle. (I later learned that the back

side of the knife blade was used, with lipstick preplaced to leave the red mark, so no real cut was made. But it sure scared the crap out of those of us not in the know!)

As Meteu continued around the circle, he and Chief Allowat Sakima did the same "tap out" for each candidate until they had all been removed from the group gathered to begin their Ordeal and night alone in the wilderness. As the tom-tom

Good friends Pete Mikel as Meteu and Chuck Campbell as Allowat Sakima

beat more softly, we were solemnly dismissed. The fire was glowing orange with coals and beginning to collapse upon itself as it silhouetted the procession filing silently back to our campsites to ponder the significance and symbolism of the ceremony. This campfire experience was something truly remarkable for me—something reverent that bestowed great honor on those selected. I wasn't certain of how I could come to belong to this special "Brotherhood of Cheerful Service" but I knew after that night that it was something that I desperately wanted.

As I reflect now on that night and ask myself why it had such a strong and lasting impact, I know it was significant because of its ceremony. The individuals being honored were being singled out and separated from the larger body in a very public way visible to the entire body. Many societies the world over still have similar manhood ceremonies today, where boys are called out to become men. This tradition is something that we have lost, or perhaps never had, in our western society here in the U.S. There is no day that any young man can point to and say, "That is the day that my father allowed me to call other men by their first name or the day my mother began treating me differently than as a child."

A BOY NEEDS A DAY HE CAN POINT TO AND SAY, "THIS IS WHEN I BECAME A MAN."

Genuine and authentic manhood cries out for such a ceremony, a time where we all "Meet the Medicine Man." This needs to be a time where preparation and careful attention are given to make it memorable and special. As is always the case, with rights come responsibilities. This ceremony should be marked as a day that peers and parents point to as a reminder that you are to act differently as a young man than you did as a child. You have been marked reverently as a new adult!

CHAPTER FOUR

SUBMITTING TO AUTHORITY

I returned to Camp Sol Mayer for the next three years, earning merit badges like rifle and shotgun shooting, rowing, and reptile study. I progressed through the ranks as fast as I possibly could to achieve the rank of Eagle Scout before age sixteen when my older brother, Richard, received his. I received my Eagle Scout Certificate on September 18, 1975, my fifteenth birthday.

By 1975 I had been elected to the Order of the Arrow and had also moved from Ordeal to Brotherhood membership rank. I was quite impressed with and developed a deep respect for Native American culture. They wasted nothing, respected their elders, and were very closely integrated with nature in every way. In 1976 I accepted a job to work on staff at both summer camps, Camp Sol Mayer on the San Saba

River and Camp Fawcett, along the crystal-clear Nueces River near Uvalde Texas further south. By this time, I was also Chapter Chief and Vice Lodge Chief for the Wahinkto Lodge of the Order of the Arrow (this was the lodge with the same geography as the Concho Valley Council). This position meant that I would play the part of Chief Allowat Sakima in the weekly tap out ceremonies that summer at both camps.

1974 Life Service Project Goodfellow AFB Scout Hut (Left Gaylord King, Right David Savage)

In the summer of 1976, I made $30 a week and lived in a wall tent on top of a wooden platform with Gary Ray, my fellow waterfront boating merit badge instructor. Our boss, the Waterfront Director, was a colorful character named Richard Gill. Richard was 21 years old, a requirement for the Waterfront Director position, but had no real scouting background. He had the same name as my older brother and was six years my elder. There was a seven-year gap between my brother and me, so the similarities made our relationship easy and natural for me.

Richard drove a gold 1973 Pontiac Grand Prix that had the longest hood of any car I had ever seen. Under that long hood was a very powerful engine—because that car could flat out haul ass! Howard Weathersby, a fellow swim team member from my high school, rounded out our quartet on the waterfront. I was the rowing merit badge instructor, Gary was the instructor for the canoeing merit badge, Howard for the swimming merit badge, and Richard for the lifesaving merit badge. At both camps, our tents were down by the San Saba and Nueces Rivers apart from the rest of the staff enclave. Our tent location was because we wore bathing suits to teach the merit badges throughout the day, yet we had to wear dress uniforms to all meals in the dining hall, which also meant changing clothes multiple times a day. The remainder of the camp staff had to wear their dress uniforms constantly. Regulation attire included a scout uniform shirt with a staff neckerchief, scout uniform shorts with belt, knee socks with colored tab garters, appropriate footwear, and a staff hat. We felt elitist on the waterfront since we were the only staff not to have the "Staff Knee" tan line. Between the high socks and long shorts, there was a band, about five or six inches wide, right around the knee, which was the only part of their legs that were constantly in the sun. The result was a tanned knee band, which looked quite peculiar when swimming.

Our waterfront quartet became quite the tight little squad under Richard's gregarious leadership. As high school teenagers, the three of us who reported to him were rapt listeners to his girl-chasing stories and other tall tales of young adult life. The other thing about our close-knit unit was our common delight in pranks and practical jokes on other staff members and campers to a lesser degree. We would routinely turn the big bell at the dining hall upside down overnight and fill it with water. Every morning the chief cook had to walk out and ring the bell to summon everyone to breakfast and never remembered to look up before yanking on the rope to ring the bell. A sudden dump of several gallons of water often led to a loud curse following the first clang of the bell.

Camp Sol Mayer Dining Hall (bell is not visible)

When it came to our campers, we had to be much more careful with any practical jokes since we were staff and official representatives of the BSA. But there were those boys who just begged to be taught a small lesson for which there was no appropriate merit badge. As a recovering mischief-maker myself, I knew them well and recognized their motive—attention seeking! Since we taught all of our waterfront merit badges on natural rivers, we decided to invent a bizarre new disease just for these special boys. It was always deep into the week but still a day or two before camp was over when one of us would carefully examine the ears of the subject. With great concern and alarm, we would announce that they **had it! Earlobe-itis!** A strange skin infection transmitted by unseen bacteria in the rivers. We would wait for them to beg us for the treatment to get rid of it. There was only one successful treatment: we needed to paint their ears with the old orange Merthiolate Tincture (an orange mercury-based dye for disinfection). We derived great humor every time we saw one of our subjects at campfires, in the dining hall, or around camp in general. That orange dye did not wash off! Those bright orange ears could be easily spotted at great distances and would last for days.

It all came to a crashing halt, however, after a furious letter from a parent was received once their child got home and they heard about our fictitious disease and its treatment. It was harmless, and we thought we were providing a solution to the attention these boys so desperately wanted. Our Camp Director, Frank Hilton, was less amused.

Our weekly routine as a staff was to welcome new campers each Sunday and send them off the following Saturday morning. This schedule would give us one night off each week to head into town for a burger or game of pool. Feeling emboldened by Richard's coaching and exhortations to try out new conversational skills with members of the opposite sex, we would head to Craig's General Store and Restaurant in Camp Wood, the tiny little town near Camp Fawcett. We had learned that Mr. Craig had four teenage daughters who worked in the store and restaurant. Every scout on staff competed for their attention as the only prey around. We would be extremely polite and courteous and even help them mop floors or do other chores so that we could be one of the lucky four they might have a Coke® with after they got off duty. I remember vividly how my competitive instinct took over all other thought processes and how triumphant I felt when I secured the position as winning suitor with the daughter who was also a sophomore to be in the coming fall school year. When I got back to San Angelo after summer camp, we wrote for a couple of months, but when she sent me her school photo that fall, I realized that what drove me was much more about winning the competition with the other boys for her attention than her attractiveness.

1976 was the country's Bicentennial Anniversary. America turned two hundred years old! Throughout the entire year, there were many patriotic activities, and we expected the Fourth of July to be the best ever in terms of celebrations and fireworks. Nearly all of June was at Camp Sol Mayer near Ft McKavett, but on the first of July, we moved to Camp Fawcett, which was not far from Garner State Park, a popular spot in that part of the state on the Frio River. With celebrations at

Garner State Park and rodeos in Rock Springs, we had high hopes for more chances at meeting more small-town girls on our Saturday nights off.

We had one chore each Saturday before we could take off. We were responsible for hosting the WEBLOS, boys about to graduate from Cub Scouts to Boy Scouts, who would come out for the day only on Saturdays to earn a few skill awards. All of them wanted to learn to row, and I was responsible for teaching them. The boating area on the Nueces River at Camp Fawcett was below a thirty-foot bluff where we would store the boats well above the water when they were not in use. We didn't have a dock or any structures down at the water level, so we would just pull the rowboats and canoes up onto the gravel shoals for short term breaks and meals. Each day at the end of instruction, we would recruit the boys and leaders to help haul the rowboats and canoes up the bluff for overnight storage.

The Saturday of the big Bicentennial Fourth of July Weekend, the WEBLOS took off, and I had no one to help me haul the rowboats, which were considerably heavier than the canoes, up the bluff. I was eager to go purchase a gross of bottle rockets for our planned war among staff members at a nearby low water crossing along the remote highway, so I just pulled the six rowboats up the gravel shoal as far as I could, tied them together, and left for the Rock Springs rodeo with my Waterfront companions. We had a great time at the rodeo and then conducted a spectacular bottle rocket and roman candle war across the low water crossing laying on our bellies on either side of the embankment. We began to see a lot of lightning off in the distance and decided to head back to camp before the approaching storm caught us.

Weary from the full day of activities and excitement, we retired to our tents as the rain began to come down, at first in a light pitter-patter, but then in sideways sheets wobbling the wall tent like a bellows for a blacksmith. Gary and I fell asleep quickly, listening to the storm and hoping our tent would hold up. A few hours later, we were suddenly awakened by the flaps of our tent being thrown wide open and a very bright flashlight shining in our faces. It was Frank Hilton, the Camp Director, standing in the still-driving rain with a poncho on and a grave look on his face.

"David!" He said sharply. "Wake Up! Where are the rowboats?"

Confused and groggy, I mumbled something back and then realized that we had not carried them up the bluff. Not waiting for an intelligible answer, Frank shouted over the storm,

"Get your ponchos on and come with me!"

"Yes, sir!" we both said as we jumped up, pulling our ponchos on over our heads.

We followed Frank swiftly with our flashlights to the edge of the bluff in the driving rain. Just a few hours before, we were looking down thirty feet to the water level on a hot, lazy Fourth of July afternoon. Now the water was a raging torrent only a few feet from the top of the bluff. I instantly got a sick feeling in my stomach as I knew the rowboats had been washed away by the rising river. I told Frank what had happened with the WEBLOS and what I was sure had happened. He was furious with me!

I INSTANTLY GOT A SICK FEELING IN MY STOMACH AS I KNEW THE ROWBOATS HAD BEEN WASHED AWAY BY THE RISING RIVER.

"How could you be so irresponsible?"

He spun around to get Richard and Howard out of their tent, and then the five of us piled in his Carryall vehicle to head down to a low water crossing a few miles downstream to try to intercept the rowboats there. We roped up and watched the swift water flowing over the road about knee-deep. We each had a bright lantern flashlight that we were sweeping the river upstream with looking for signs of our rowboats. We saw one coming toward us!

We slid our feet along the road, roped together, and tried to lasso, catch, pull or by some other means get hold of the swamped rowboat. This plan was insane and seemed extremely dangerous to me, but scout camp resources were scarce, and these were valuable and essential to summer camp. Frank knew our strengths and skills and must have believed in us tremendously as a unit to put us in this situation. Cars and trucks had been waiting for the river to drop from both directions on the road and their headlights helped us see better and position ourselves as safely as possible for when the rowboats came down. At one point, a man pulling a horse trailer coming from the rodeo in Rock Springs we had attended decided he would try to cross in the swift water. We begged and pleaded with him not to try it. His truck clearance was not high enough to keep the rapid river from hitting the body of the truck and the trailer broadside. He ignored us, rolling up his window and gunning the engine to advance into the water. We could only helplessly watch as he got out to the deepest part where the trailer jack-knifed, and both the truck and the trailer were swept down the river and out of the reach of our flashlight beams. There was nothing we could have done once they were downriver, and it remains a riveting memory today about the power of flash floods. We learned the next day that both the driver and the horse had drowned.

One by one, we retrieved five of the rowboats, catching them at the low water crossing that night. The next morning, Frank was still hot and chewing me out about how irresponsible I was for not finding someone to help drag the rowboats up the bluff when I had finished with the WEBLOS. He then demanded that Howard and I use one of the canoes and go down the river to try to find the missing rowboat, which must have gone by before we got to the low water crossing. We were standing in a sea of mud with our ponchos on, and the river still quite high and dangerous. I had had enough of his lectures, living in a tent, and risking my life for his damned rowboats—and I told him so!

"Frank, you pay me $30 a week to live in a tent and change clothes six times a day! We watched a man and his horse drown last night after we had been taking huge risks to catch rowboats in the middle of the night at that low water crossing, and you can just shove that last rowboat where the sun never shines! I QUIT!"

Frank's eyes narrowed, and he became much sterner than I had ever seen him.

"Now look here, David, every time you think you are indispensable, stick your finger in a glass of water, pull it out, and see how big a hole it leaves! Now get the canoe and go get that last rowboat!"

I was sixteen and still respected this man tremendously, and he had just called my bluff. I was either going after the boat, or I was going to have to hike about 180 miles to get back to San Angelo. After a long and thoughtful pause, for effect only, I said, "Yes, sir! I'll grab Howard, and we will go after that last rowboat!"

It was actually quite fun canoeing the river in a high flow condition, and since it was all downstream, it went fast with mostly just steering through debris and

Frank Hilton and me forty years later—still friends in touch

trees that had caved in from the banks. That is where we found the final rowboat, tangled up in a half-submerged tree. The seat had been knocked out of position, and there were some superficial dents, but it was still serviceable. We towed it behind our canoe to the next bridge, and Frank came with the boat trailer to pick us up. That "indispensable" speech was one I have never forgotten. I have used it many times throughout my career with employees who seemed to value themselves a bit too highly. But my real lesson from that experience was in obedience.

Calmer Nueces River Waterfront at Camp Fawcett

CHAPTER FIVE

STRETCHING THE HORIZON

At age fifteen to sixteen, young men are growing physically stronger, their voice is getting deeper, and for some, whiskers are even sprouting on their faces. There is an innate and gnawing desire inside to find out if he has what it takes to be a man, to test himself against the elements or perhaps other young men in a competition of some kind. There is also a strong desire to break away from mom and seek more time with dad to explore his family's definition of masculinity. It is an important time to stretch his horizons and press against the limits of his boyhood strength, endurance, and fears.

In 1976, the hunger for more adventure was calling me to another level of scouting beyond summer camp and merit badges. I had seen the famous arrowhead patches and heard others talk about Philmont Scout Ranch in the Sangre de Christo mountain range near Cimarron, New Mexico. It was the penultimate scouting experience. It was called a High Adventure Base with a minimum age requirement of fourteen. With 214 square miles of terrain, it is the largest BSA National High Adventure Base, with elevation ranging from 6,500 to 12,441 feet. Crews, as they are called at Philmont, sign up for one of several ten-day itineraries called treks. These treks crisscross the ranch, and campers backpack from one backcountry camp to another where various programs are offered. These camps have staff who live in the backcountry all summer and run the programs offered at each location. These programs offer the best of the Old West like horseback riding, burro packing, gold panning, chuckwagon dinners, and interpretative history. They also offer exciting challenges such as rock climbing, black powder rifle shooting, and lumberjack skills.

The allure of just being in the mountains was tremendous, but the opportunity to experience the Old West lifestyle firsthand, shoot black powder rifles, and learn technical rock climbing made Philmont irresistible to me! Getting on a Philmont crew and funding the trip became my singular ambition for the summer, and the primary reason I worked on camp staff in June and July.

When my job on staff at summer camp was over, I had saved enough money to meet my contribution requirements. My parents covered the rest so that I could go to Philmont with a Scoutmaster and a few of the boys from his troop in Fort Stockton, Texas, which was also in the Concho Valley Council. There were a couple of other boys I knew well from San Angelo troops who also joined up for our total ten-member crew as a kind of all-star team from our Council.

Philmont as a camper in August of 1976 (standing third from right)

I was elated to actually travel to some mountains in an adjacent state and experience the Old West in a personal way. We drove from San Angelo to Cimarron, New Mexico, and had some root beers at an old historic hotel where there were actual bullet holes still in the wall from a genuine shootout with outlaws!

Upon arriving at Philmont itself, we were greeted by our assigned Ranger. The Ranger's job is to meet the crew, review their physicals, give them a shakedown on their gear, and generally orient them to base camp. We followed him to the commissary and picked up our first allotment of dehydrated meals for our ten-day trek and then attended a welcome campfire for all of the crews coming in that week.

The Philmont reputation and experience are well-known among scouting circles as the very best that the BSA has to offer. I learned that 20,000 applications are received each year for only several hundred

Ranger positions, so the competition for a coveted position truly anywhere on the staff was fierce and demanded the very finest scouting credentials. The most noticeable thing we all observed as soon as we arrived at Philmont was how friendly every staff person was.

We were briefed on another popular activity—patch trading. At Philmont, crews were attending from all over the country as well as a few international groups. Once we got scattered across the ranch backpacking on the trails, we wouldn't see them much, so if you wanted to make a trade, you had to strike while the opportunity was hot! The basic trading stock was the Council Shoulder Patch (CSP), identifying your Council. If you were in Order of the Arrow, you had the more limited and coveted OA Lodge Flap worn on the pocket flap over the right breast pocket. Belt buckles, neckerchiefs, and all sorts of other trading took place from vials of Texas crude oil to rattlesnake skins from our part of the country to buckeyes from Ohio or macadamia nuts from Hawaii. This commerce fascinated me as I watched the barter process unfold in small groups throughout the base camp. I had purchased thirty CSP's from our council trading post. It was a brand-new edition, so no one had one yet. The highest value was placed on a fully embroidered patch and then mostly on its attractiveness. Next in value was whatever a person needed to complete some portion of their collection. Our patch was a silhouette of a black oil pump jack, a yucca cactus, and an antlered buck with a West Texas sunset with orange, red, and yellow behind them. It was a strikingly attractive patch and was considered part of a "shadow set" with other silhouette style patches from other councils.

Trading was an area to test myself against my peers in negotiation skills. The size of the deal was limited only by your own imagination, and the key was in asking questions to find out what your trading partner truly valued most. This exercise was another early indicator of a talent I possessed for my work to do. It also gave me early practice of a skill that would guide my career later in life in large contract negotiations in the Energy industry.

Once we hit the trail, our Ranger was with us for the first three days training us on how to impact the wilderness and camping areas minimally to reduce bear and other animal encounters with the human population. After the first three days, it becomes the Senior Patrol Leader's responsibility to lead the crew, read the map, and generally make most of the decisions with minimal adult involvement. This is why scouting is so valuable; it gives young men training in leadership and lets them experience the consequences in a safe environment (i.e., not reading a map well can cost you a lot of extra miles hiking and make you unpopular with your crew).

We did the backcountry camps at Apache Springs where we learned about Apache sweat lodges, archery, and making arrowheads; we shot fifty caliber balls with black powder rifles and learned about blacksmithing at Black Mountain; we learned all about roping up and rock climbing at Cimarroncito; and we learned about prospecting and gold mining at Cypher's Mine. Our most memorable moment came at Cypher's Mine, where we stayed in Adirondack shelters totally open on one side rather than in our tents. The area had been getting hit by a six-hundred-pound female black bear they had named Lula Bell with her two cubs. We were extra vigilant in hanging our bear bags with all of our food and "smellables" like toothpaste and Chapstick. The guidance is to hang these bags at least ten feet off the ground and eight feet from any tree trunk between two large trees. We did this with a large amount of food for a crew of ten. Our fire had burned down to embers, and we were all just falling asleep in the shelter when we began to hear loud cracking of branches and low bear noises. We all popped out of sleeping bags to discover Lula Bell standing on her hind legs, pawing the bottom of the bags open and spilling all the food onto the ground. No one was going to set a single foot outside of the shelter, so we grabbed our pots and utensils and pounded on them as loud as we could while yelling at the top of our lungs to try to scare her off. She was oblivious to this tactic, and as we swept our flashlight beams around, we saw her accomplices; the two cubs were in one of the trees trying to yank the rope knots out! These bears knew what they were doing!

Some of us stepped out of the shelter far enough to whiz a few rocks at the cubs, against our leader's advice. One hit the mark, and the cub tumbled down from the tree, and the other quickly followed. Fortunately, they were not hurt and ran away up the hill but not before they and their mother had dragged most of our food up the hill with them.

It was like a keystone cops skit with boys running all around the small area of light that the embers from the fire provided, picking up tiny twigs and throwing them on the embers to provide a larger perimeter of light. This process was repeated several times until we had the fire going good and considerably more light with which to work. Our leader, Roy Armstrong, took a couple of us up the hill slightly to see what they got off with and what we might be able to retrieve. We could still hear the bears crashing around nearby in the woods and wisely decided that they could have whatever they wanted from what was beyond our immediate reach. We would happily hike the extra miles to a backcountry commissary to resupply ourselves the next day rather than tangle with a mother bear and her two adolescent cubs.

It was probably the most exhilarating moment in each of our young lives thus far. I recall how hard my heart was pounding and the feeling of adrenaline instantly waking us all up once we began hearing noises. We found one of the other boys' cameras with a big tooth hole in it and a canteen with Gatorade in it punctured in several places by claws.

Another boy had forgotten a package of hot chocolate in an outer pocket on his pack, and it was ripped off with bear snot all over it. We had survived a bear encounter, and it was like a special forces merit badge and superb memory of valor for all of us. This is exactly why we had come to Philmont!

WE HAD SURVIVED A BEAR ENCOUNTER, AND IT WAS LIKE A SPECIAL FORCES MERIT BADGE AND SUPERB MEMORY OF VALOR FOR ALL OF US.

The following year I went to the 1977 National Jamboree in Moraine State Park, Pennsylvania to stretch my horizon even farther. The most memorable part of that trip was a multiday period in Washington, D.C., where we got to meet our Congressman, Robert Krueger, and our Senator, Lloyd Bentson, as we toured the House and Senate Chambers. We saw the Smithsonian Museum and the National Archives as well as the many monuments around the mall. The most impactful event of all for me was called The Evening Parade at the United States Marine Barracks. I still have the program where it states:

> *The Barracks has been the home of the United States Marine Band, "the President's Own" since 1801. The legendary John Phillip Sousa, when he was the leader of the Band, wrote many of his famous marches here.*

As a drum major back in ninth grade, I was very keen on marching band drills. Being an Air Force brat, where we heard the National Anthem played daily from our backyard adjacent to the base, also made me an extremely patriotic young man. This group of marines was so precise and sharp in both their musicianship and marching maneuvers, I was simply blown away by their performance. It still gives me chills to think of it!

Janet Miller and David Savage
Edison Junior High 1975

Scouting gave me these opportunities to stretch my horizon, to test myself against the elements as we experienced torrential rain and lightning at the National Jamboree throughout the week, and to encounter bears in the wild and live to tell the tale. I took an aptitude exam at the National Jamboree and won a full scholarship to Carnegie Melon University. I was totally unfamiliar with this fine university in Pennsylvania, and I tossed the letter in the trash when I received my award notification because I was afraid to go out of state to college at that time. I was learning, growing, and making mistakes—all necessary steps along the path through the wilderness to manhood.

Standing seventh from left is Patrol Leader
Savage in Moraine State Park, PA

CHAPTER SIX

LOYALTY VERSUS LADIES

I believe God has three common purposes for every man: find a work to do, a woman to love, and a will to obey. Adolescence is an important sojourn in the pursuit of these purposes on the crossing from boy to man. It is a time to wander into the wildest wilderness of all—girls. At sixteen, I was growing increasingly interested in the adventure of finding a woman to love.

There are voices out there, suggesting that our gender is somehow optional. That is just a flat out lie. We are created as sexual beings and are born either male or female; if you wonder about that, just look down the front of your pants. It's pretty clear. As sexual beings, we have been hard-wired to procreate in order to continue our species. This reality is no different than every other warm-blooded mammal on the planet. We cannot deny the natural world or how we are part of it with these qualities mapped into our DNA. Our distinction from the rest of the animal world is that God gave us reason in addition to instinct. An animal uses its senses and acts instantly out of instinct in dangerous situations. We have instincts, too, but are less aware of them as our brains have developed much more to the reasoning side of the equation. Again, instincts don't wait for thought or calculation; you just react. The fight or flight instinct is perhaps the best-known example.

Now when it comes to the hormone-enhanced world of being a teenager, we are all experiencing an evolutionary battle that all of our ancestors experienced as well. It is the battle between our instinct and our intellect. In my case, I was fortunate to have two wonderful and loving older sisters, in addition to my mother, as members of the opposite sex living in my household. I understood that they were not perfect, that they could irritate me, and that they were indeed quite different than my brother, father, and me. I have friends who grew up with only brothers and a mother who they never saw without her hair done and makeup on. They have related stories to me of their complete bewilderment with the opposite sex for most of their early lives.

For most of human history in all cultures, marriage was arranged. There was a stratification of society where one could not pass between different social classes. Dowries were required as payment from the family of the young woman. Partners were chosen to consolidate growing power through closer family ties. All of the monarchies of Europe are good examples of this from history. I have friends from India who are in marriages today, which were arranged by their families. I have been very curious about the contrast between our cultures because their system seems to work better than ours in terms of the marriage lasting. My own theory is that this is due to the fact that arranged marriages significantly reduce the role of glands in the decision and elevate the role of compatibility and commonality. In other words, they are assuring a greater collective amount of intellect weighted against a lesser amount of instinct or the pure chemistry of attraction.

The United States isn't known as the home of the Wild West for nothing. So here I was, sixteen years old, growing hair in new places, playing clarinet in the band with one other guy and about twenty young ladies, listening to stories from my older brother, Richard Savage, and my Waterfront Director, Richard Gill, and being challenged by both to follow my glands and check out my relational skills. The fact that I looked up to both of these twenty-something role models made them very influential, but the most important male figure of my life was my father, and he was strangely silent on this topic. Let me pause here to state unequivocally that if you are a father reading this, you MUST be the educator on this topic. Please do not leave your sons and daughters to stumble around on the internet or to be swayed by foolish and reckless peers! Your children are struggling as it is between instinct and intellect, and neither is fully developed yet. I'll step down from my soapbox now so we can return to my journey.

After the summer of 1976, working at boy scout camps and going to Philmont for high adventure, I decided that in 1977 I would use my swimming and lifesaving skills to apply for a job as a lifeguard at Goodfellow Air Force Base. The pay was better than scout camp, and the employment was for the full summer. I was also becoming a competitive diver on the swim team at school and wanted to practice that sport more. I landed the job and worked with older lifeguards who I had known well from previous summers. I was a well-known pool rat and splash dive specialist—perfectly executed to get the female lifeguards wet when they had to sit up in the stand—so I fit in well with the staff as a new recruit. It was a fun summer, where I also learned to do everything mechanically to manage the pool itself and keep it clean and treated.

Showing off the muscles and diving skills

I graduated from high school the following summer in 1978 and was given even greater opportunities to learn. The older crew did not return, and I was asked to be the pool manager by the Morale, Welfare, and Recreation Dept. This job meant that I would be responsible for the two pools on the base, one for the officers and one for the NCOs (non-commissioned officers). I was also in charge of hiring the ten other lifeguards to be on staff that summer. I made a HUGE mistake! I hired nine of the best-looking girls I knew and one of my best male friends. I ended up firing my good buddy for being intoxicated at work, which kind of soured our friendship for a while, and I spent the entire summer refereeing catfights between the girls, most of whom only wanted to tan and not work. However, one story stands out as a real example of the battle between my instinct and my intellect.

Most of the enlisted men stationed at Goodfellow AFB were about the same age as me, just out of high school and enlisting in the military for various reasons rather than going to college. These guys were all smart because the school at GAFB was for the intelligence jobs in cryptology and linguistics. When you enlist in the military, they want to get everyone on the same level, so they shave your head, issue uniforms, and do as much as they can to remove individuality. All these guys were young, athletic, had shaved heads, and were even issued the same standard white government issue swim trunks. There was one very notable exception to the new class of students; an extremely attractive young woman named JoAnn who came to the pool quite regularly to sun and read her books.

In 1978, Cover Girl Makeup was quite popular, and all of the up-and-coming supermodels were the ones on the boxes of their products on the shelves in stores, in magazine ads, and in television commercials. Cheryl Tiegs was the primary spokesperson at the time, and she wore a white one-piece bathing suit with green polka dots in all of those ads. JoAnn wore the same bathing suit on many occasions, and in the estimation of most of us around the pool was every bit as fetching as Cheryl Tiegs. The group would exhort each of the young Air Force recruits one-by-one to make an advance on JoAnn. Each and every time, they were shot down in flames.

As the Head Lifeguard and Pool Manager, I was simply an observer of these sorties over a period of several weeks. These guys were my buddies, and they were taking the public rejection pretty hard. She was a total "Snuff Queen," as we used to say in West Texas. She would systematically snuff out any hopes they might have had for even a conversation, let alone a date. Those guys were my friends, and I did not like the way she was treating them. Perhaps they were all competing for a very small number of exclusive assignments once their training was finished, or perhaps, she knew they would all be transferred to different locales around the world, so why begin a new relationship? It didn't matter to me. I had judged her as cold as ice, and I would not give her the satisfaction of adding me as "another notch in her lipstick case," as the Pat Benatar song says. But I could not totally suppress my instincts either. I found her extremely attractive, just like everyone else.

Most days, I would take a fifteen-minute break to practice my diving before climbing up in the stand for my shift. I was an above-average diver and maybe the best in my town of 90,000 people, so I confess that I was a showoff. I knew that JoAnn always watched me closely. I would do handstand dives and hold the handstand for as long as I could to make sure I had as much attention as possible. One day after an excellent diving session of clean entries after flips and twists, I climbed up into the stand with my Ray-Ban® mirrored sunglasses on and began my shift. Low and behold, JoAnn came up to me at the side of the lifeguard stand. My male Air Force friends were incredulous. She knew my name; I guess from overhearing conversations for weeks. She slowly raised her sunglasses to reveal her magnificent eyes and softly asked,

"David, where did you learn to dive like that?"

I was melting like butter inside; true warfare was taking place between my instinct and my intellect, but my loyalty to my friends won the day, and my intellect and reasoning prevailed. I thought to myself, *"This gorgeous creature needs a little taste of her own medicine."*

I just looked at her silently with my sunglasses still mirroring her own reflection and simply pointed to the sign mounted on the side of the lifeguard stand "**PLEASE DO NOT TALK TO LIFEGUARD WHILE ON DUTY.**" To say that she was indignant would be the apex of understatement. She quickly spun on her heel and returned to her lounge with sun hat on, sunglasses down, and nose placed firmly in her book.

National Jamboree shirt with Philmont belt—always a loyal scout!

The hero's welcome I received from the other young men once she left for the day was exalting. It was like watching a football game where the underdog somehow manages the perfect game to beat the heavily favored champion with an under matched squad. It was so satisfying for them to see her get a taste of her own medicine, but this was to become just the first skirmish in a summerlong war. JoAnn was a formidable adversary with an arsenal of weapons. Plus, she was simply hypnotizing to look at! She approached me again when I wasn't in the stand and asked, "David, why don't you like me? You don't even know me."

"JoAnn," I said, "that's not true. I am just a professional who takes his job seriously."

"Then why don't you ever try to talk to me like all the other guys you run around with?"

"They are here for recreation. I am here to work and manage the pool and staff."

"Then why don't we do something after you get off some time?"

Again, in my mind, "What? She's asking me out?! This is incredible! Of course! ... No! Wait! It's a trap! Once you show any weakness, she will torch you all the more just like the others!"

I was so conflicted between instinct and intellect. I could not believe she was legitimately interested in me. This is often the case with extremely attractive women. Most men, the same age anyway, are awestruck by their beauty and just don't feel worthy of the beauty queen. JoAnn pressed her case all summer, flirting and writing me notes. She really was very hard to resist! But there was a safer bet that was almost as important to me—the loyalty and admiration of my friends. JoAnn was the forbidden fruit, the temptress who would betray me. I used my reason to place the loyalty of my friends over something so temporal, which I knew would end once she received her orders in a few weeks. I've thought back on that summer and JoAnn more than a few times, wondering, "What if?" but I think we both enjoyed the game. She was beautiful, smart, and intelligent, and I was never rude or unkind to her. My sisters gave me a little insight on most women they knew the same age: "They want what they can't have. No one values something that comes too easily or for free."

I wish to emphasize the importance of intellect when it comes to choosing the woman to love in your life. In our teen years and early twenties, we are strongly pulled by our primal instincts and raw chemistry. We need to encourage young men to seek

WHEN IT COMES TO WOMEN, WE ARE STRONGLY PULLED BY OUR PRIMAL INSTINCTS AND RAW CHEMISTRY, BUT IT IS REALLY IMPORTANT TO INVOKE YOUR INTELLECT IN THE CHOOSING PROCESS.

out their fathers or other older men they admire and look up to and ask them these questions:

- "How did you go about your own search for a woman to love?"

- "What kind of criteria should I have?"

- "What are the red flag warning signs that there is some dealbreaker quality or issue?

- "What patterns or warning signs should I look for in her family of origin?"

I mention these questions because though I chose loyalty over the ladies in this story, I was an abysmal failure later in life. In a later chapter, I will cover the big backtrack I was required to make in order to find my woman to truly love. I wish I had better guidance during my youth, and I am now committed to helping other young men see the big picture and not mistake pure physical attraction for more enduring qualities that will stand the test of time.

KEEP THE BIG PICTURE IN
MIND. DON'T MISTAKE PURE
PHYSCIAL ATTRACTION
FOR MORE ENDURING
QUALITIES THAT WILL
STAND THE TEST OF TIME.

TAKING DEAD AIM

A young man's senior year of high school is typically the most carefree period of his life. You have many privileges and few responsibilities. You have a driver's license and likely a car, yet you still live at home where your parents are providing for all of your basic needs. You are the oldest and most popular in high school, with a significant amount of independence. When I was a senior in high school, the drinking age was still eighteen, so many seniors could drink and vote. The most important thing you needed to do was to "take dead aim" as Harvey Penick, the famous golf instructor, exhorts his students. It was time to determine your "work to do" in life. That could mean trade school like automobile repair, joining the military and serving your country, or deciding what you would study in college and determining how you would fund higher education.

This decision could be severely clouded by a serious girlfriend at home as you had pursued your "woman to love" and did not want to leave that relationship to go off to school. She could be going off herself, perhaps to a different school. It was a time to set priorities and define your future path as an independent adult in the wilderness we call society.

In the last chapter, I explained how I resisted the beguiling charm of JoAnn, the attractive Air Force student. I was more vulnerable with a tall, slender, athletic blond track athlete named Katie, who also was one of the young ladies I hired on staff as a lifeguard at the base pools. Her father was an FBI agent, and her grandmother had been my elementary school principal dispensing corporal punishment on my backside with her paddle. As my first serious relationship, I was totally smitten and unreserved in my love for her. We met in a sandlot touch football game with all of my male friends back in the Spring. I came into the huddle, and they told me to cover the tall blond girl. When I asked, "Why is she even playing with us?" One of my teammates said, "Because she is fast and can play as well as any of us!"

I kind of harumphed at the notion and agreed to cover her and deny the ball to her at all costs.

She was quite fast and made a few jackrabbit moves, and the quarterback threw the ball to her coming out of her break. I dove with all I had to knock the ball away and landed on her as we both tumbled to the ground. One of the other guys said, "Hey, Savage, this is touch, not tackle!"

I replied, "If she's out here playing with the guys, she should expect to be treated like one."

She didn't say a word. She simply jumped up, brushed herself off, and went back to her team's huddle. The very next play, she burned me deep for a touchdown, and I knew that I needed to get to know this girl better.

As we worked together through the summer, we spent all of our waking time with each other and became quite serious. She was going to stay in San Angelo and attend Angelo State University on a track scholarship. I had received an Opportunity Awards Scholarship to Texas A&M University, among other offers in music to an array of schools. This situation is where working with Bob Kamensky at scout camp had a very big impact on me. He was the medicine man in the photo in chapter three back in 1976, and we had gotten to know one other well on camp staff. He was in incredible shape, and each night would do seventy-nine pushups and sets of seventy-nine sit-ups and

other calisthenics. When I asked him why seventy-nine and not eighty or one hundred, he said that he was in the Corps of Cadets at Texas A&M, Class of '79, so they were required to do this all year when in school. Bob was studying Nuclear Engineering and wanted me to be his protégé, following in his footsteps in the same major and recruiting me to consider joining the Corps and, eventually, the Navy as a career. My dad and older brother Rick were both in the Air Force and did not recommend a military career while Jimmy Carter was president.

The Medicine Man, Corps Commander Robert Kamensky, as himself in 1979

I went to San Antonio, Texas, to meet with Navy recruiters to investigate their pitch. It was quite appealing! They were fit and good looking in their white dress uniforms and painted a picture of life at sea traveling the world and pulling into ports where all the ladies swooned over young men in uniform. I declared Nuclear Engineering as my major and awaited the big ROTC scholarship results I was hoping to be awarded. I got runner up. After discussing the military life with my dad and brother, and against my mother's wishes (who thought I needed more discipline), I decided not to join the Corps. I did like Texas A&M and remained in Nuclear Engineering but would become a civilian engineer when I finished.

I tried commuting the six-hour drive back to San Angelo to see my sweetheart Katie as often as I could, but we drifted. I knew we were heading in different directions, and when I came home for Christmas after the first fall semester, I was summarily dumped and given my senior ring back. I kept a stiff upper lip externally but was devastated by the loss inside. When I returned to A&M in January, it rained twenty-nine out of thirty-one days that month and I found myself in a total funk. I hardly cared about my grades but was able to sleepwalk through the Spring semester, simmering about how I had been betrayed. It was time for me to take dead aim. I could not afford to be distracted by the opposite sex. I was on a mission. I had been fortunate enough to receive a great scholarship and get out of San Angelo, and I was no longer going to let anything deter me from my mission. This single-mindedness of purpose was not a bad thing except for how cold I became to any young woman for whom I began to have any feelings. I would inexplicably drop contact and even be intentionally rude to avoid being vulnerable to hurt again. This was a wilderness I wanted no part of, and in the end, it led me to stagnate in my emotional development, which cost me dearly later.

An event of international significance also happened that Spring. On March 29, 1979 there was a partial meltdown of reactor number two of Three Mile Island Nuclear Generating Station in Dauphin County, Pennsylvania, near Harrisburg. It is still the most significant accident in U.S. commercial nuclear power plant history. This incident blew up the nuclear industry completely, where the only job I could hope for was back on a Navy submarine. I had to recalibrate my career path and reorient my map. Most engineering students were looking at only one thing as our criteria for major selection: which discipline was capturing the highest starting salary immediately out of school. I loved water and water resources and saw that Civil Engineering was a very broad discipline that would always have a steady demand for infrastructures like roads, bridges, water, and wastewater plants. Petroleum and Chemical Engineering had higher starting salaries, but the embargo and oil price plunge of the early seventies was still pretty fresh in my mind. I chose Civil Engineering as my new major beginning the following fall.

Back home in San Angelo for the summer, I was offered my old job as pool manager at the base, and Katie had already accepted a job there again as a lifeguard. I daydreamed about being a tyrannical boss and punishing her for dumping me, but honestly, my stomach still felt ill every time I saw her. Instead, I went to the Texas Highway Department and got a job on a survey crew building roads and bridges to get civil engineering work experience. It was a far better employment decision, which helped tremendously in landing multiple job offers when I graduated. I was grateful because we were at the bottom of another oil market crash in 1982 when very few new grads were receiving any job offers at all.

In the fall semester of 1979, I began working part-time for the Civil Engineering Department conducting the Environmental Impact Study for the Strategic Petroleum Reserve. I also pledged with the Alpha Tau Omega fraternity, which had just received its Charter that semester at Texas A&M University. I had found my tribe for the remainder of my college career and made many lifelong friendships through the brotherhood of my fraternity. It felt like the fellowship I had enjoyed while working on the staff at scout camp. I also kept working at the university on the Strategic Petroleum Reserve Project until I graduated, adding to my surveying summer work at the Highway Department to build

The Delta Pledge Class of ATO Fall 1979

a strong civil engineering work history along with my education. But above all, I guarded my heart and focused on my mission—my work to do.

In the Spring of 1980, I applied for one of the coveted Ranger backpacking guide positions at Philmont, and when I received my offer letter stating that I had been chosen, I was ecstatic! It didn't pay very much, $310 a month as I recall. When I spoke with my parents, they told me I needed to earn more money because my sister, Terry, had gotten divorced and would be moving back in with her toddler and infant daughters. This news was devastating for me. Just to land the Ranger job at Philmont was extraordinarily fortunate because something like 20,000 applications come in from across the country for the less than two hundred positions. Now, I had to write Philmont and say that I would not be able to come, most likely killing any future chance of working there in the process.

How I handled this situation was an early test of true manhood. You don't have to live too long to understand that life has its disappointments. It is how we deal with them that reflects our true character. I sucked it up and returned to the survey crew at the Highway Department and tried to be there for my sister and my nieces in their hour of need. I didn't know it at the time, but my brother Rick and even my parents, after thirty-one years, would also end their marriages in divorce in the coming two years. By the time I graduated from A&M in the Spring of 1982, my very tender heart, which I had been carefully protecting, hardened to its core. This is where I began my real journey through the wilderness, and I decided I was going to do it alone.

The notion of a will to obey could only be my own will. I was a baptized and confirmed Methodist who still believed in God, but I had already stopped going to church when I went off to college. My own heart had been broken with my first true love, and now every member of my family was experiencing the pain of divorce. I was seriously questioning the goodness of God and certainly His will for my life. I was lost and on my own in the wilderness.

I WAS SERIOUSLY QUESTIONING THE GOODNESS OF GOD AND HIS WILL FOR MY LIFE—I WAS LOST AND ON MY OWN IN THE WILDERNESS.

Thinking that one of my purposes in life was to find a woman to love was the farthest possible thing from my mind as I walked across the stage to receive my degree on May 7, 1982. My father called me the day before to tell me that he and my mom would not be able to make it to my graduation due to car problems. I was totally crushed and pulled a massive drunk with some of my fraternity brothers to try to drown out the pain. I showed up at graduation, severely hungover. My mother would not have it, and they borrowed our neighbors' car to show up eventually, but the damage had been done. I could not

Texas A&M University Spring Commencement May 1982

believe that it could even have been considered to miss my graduation from Texas A&M!

As the youngest child, considerable pressure had been put on me by my parents to be a success after some severe disappointments, including the divorces of my siblings. I had observed the impact on my parents of those experiences, and I was determined to make them proud. I had already been offered four different jobs and accepted the offer as a new associate engineer for

Turner Collie & Braden Consulting Engineers in Houston, Texas. I was unaware of my parents' marriage struggles and that they were only hanging in there until I graduated. These were the days before cell phones, so I had no idea that they had borrowed a car and were on their way to College Station until they pulled up at the fraternity house where I was living and found me nearly incoherent on the couch. I had a few hours to pull myself together somewhat, but I must confess that writing about it is difficult for me even now. What should have been the proudest day of my life at that point was badly stained.

As with all dark clouds, there was a silver lining for me that deeply embedded the value of brotherhood and the family you choose. My ATO fraternity brothers were there for me when my natural family could not be. All were trying to complete their degrees and meet graduation requirements, so they fully understood and appreciated the accomplishment. They helped me get through that low point and not lose the achievement in my disappointment. Quality friendships are valuable beyond compare. Iron indeed does sharpen iron, and a friend who sticks close to you in adversity is closer than a brother. Find companions who will stand by you come what may, and you will be a man wealthy in wisdom, able to weather life's storms and emerge from them with character intact.

QUALITY FRIENDSHIPS
ARE VALUABLE
BEYOND COMPARE.

THE BEST DECISION
OF MY LIFE

As I was interviewing for engineering jobs through the Texas A&M Placement Center in the fall of 1981 and the spring of 1982, my primary search criteria was this: Did the firm have an office in Denver, Colorado? I loved the outdoors and the mountains, so I wanted to be near them wherever I took my first job. At that time, there was no limit on the number of interviews one could sign up for with the Placement Center, so I took full advantage for two reasons. First, I would interview with my second tier of job prospects initially so I could practice and become more polished. Second, the more I interviewed, the more possible offers I could have and the greater the choice of pay and location options were available. I interviewed with twenty-five firms that all had offices in Denver, Colorado. I received four job offers in hot, humid Houston, Texas—quite far from any mountains.

I could not let go of my lifelong dream to be a Philmont Ranger before I began my true career as an engineer. I knew that I would never have a full summer available again after starting an engineering career, and I was still stinging from having to write Philmont that letter back in 1980 to give up the job then. I decided I would run the Philmont trap one more time to see what they would say. I was a twenty-one-year-old college graduate with sterling scouting credentials, and they were even more eager to hire me for the summer of 1982 than back in 1980! I was so excited! I had already accepted my job offer with Turner Collie & Braden (TCB), so I needed to speak with them about my start date. I didn't know it at the time, but they had only hired two engineers that spring after interviewing across much of the country's college campuses. I would not have taken the risk of changing my start date with them if I had known that. In fact, many of my classmates who had higher GPAs than me had no job offers and were having to go on to grad school because the big oil company jobs were all dried up. My job at TCB was originally slated to be in a new office they were opening in Grand Junction, Colorado, to work on something called the shale boom. But the boom went bust, and the office was closed before it ever opened. To my delight, they were agreeable about moving my start date back to late August because of those changes.

I left Texas A&M University and College Station in mid-May of 1982 in my old 1964 Mercury Comet with very few belongings and a troubled heart. I was twenty-one and beginning my new life of adult independence as I drove across Texas alone. I only stopped in San Angelo briefly to pick up a few things and then headed further west into the old Comancheria wilderness, through the high plains along the Llano Estacado country intersecting the old Santa Fe Trail to Cimarron, New Mexico. When I pulled into the Philmont base camp, I knew no one else, and no one else knew me. I reported for duty to my new job, received my new backpack and tent, and was assigned a tent in base camp with a tentmate from Delaware in my Ranger Training Crew. I knew and loved Philmont from my experience there as a camper in 1976, and I knew that I was fortunate to be among its talented and friendly staff. This was truly the best decision of my life to take this summer to come work here and sort myself out before beginning my professional career in earnest.

My Ranger Training Crew (seated far right)

Being on staff for the most prestigious high adventure scouting experience worldwide came with high expectations. We were groomed in a staff training week to give local history, learn and be able to describe flora and fauna in several climate zones, and practice the high adventure programs like rock climbing in the backcountry camps. We were also trained on how to have a minimal impact on the land and use the sumps in established camps to minimize wild animal encounters.

The job of the ranger is to meet the crews when they arrive at Philmont. We reviewed their medical records and gave them a "shakedown" to help reduce unnecessary weight and make their hiking easier. It was then our job to train the Senior Patrol Leader, the boy selected as the crew's leader, for the first three days of their ten-day itinerary on the trail. On the morning of the third day, the ranger says goodbye and hikes back to base camp by himself to meet the next crew or have a day off in the backcountry. For the remaining week, the Senior Patrol Leader's responsibility is to navigate with map and compass and lead the crew through the remainder of the trek as they backpack from one established backcountry camp to another. I described most of those backcountry camps and programs previously in chapter five.

Of course, there was a campfire in base camp where the crews are introduced to Philmont traditions and songs and oriented on their upcoming trek. There was always a lot of emphasis on bear precautions, and I'm sure that many a boy had their senses acutely tuned after all of the bear briefings. But just being in nature tunes one's senses in the most primal parts of our brain, turning on instincts like fight or flight that we have dulled through constant stimulation from television, radio, or electronic games.

In his book titled *Whispers in the Wilderness*, Erik Stensland opens with the term "wild embrace" to describe how retreating deep into creation connects us with God and gives us the ability to hear the whispers in the wilderness. It is in the wild and beautiful places where we grow, like a snake shedding his skin, leaving behind the baggage of the world to be made new. Our hearing and sense of smell become much keener as we get farther from towns and base camp and hike the backcountry trails with our thoughts and imaginations. Odors from skunks are always strong, but you begin to notice other smells from other animals as you hike or walk along a river or lakeshore. Your heart nearly stops as, suddenly, a large grouse flushes and loudly flaps away from bushes three feet away from where you saw nothing a moment before.

In the dark, inside your tent is when your hearing is keenest because your sight is limited, and your surroundings are unfamiliar. The wind in the treetops makes them creak as they bend, and a pinecone falls onto your tent.

"What was THAT?" you ask your tentmate.

Two coyotes can sound like twenty as they howl and bark, reminding you that you are not alone. Owls hoot, and another camper snores. Twigs snap, and you hear larger game snort and sniff in the night. You feel electric and more alive than you can ever recall, and you long for that comfort, warmth, and light of the campfire. This is the part of you that connects with all of humanity and our history. It is that sense of belonging that surfaces again.

The first night out with a new crew, you take a bus ride out to the trailheads, leading to the wilderness. At the trailhead you review basic map and compass skills and lead the crew to their first overnight campsite. These are well established at Philmont with sumps, latrines, and fire rings to limit the impact to a more confined area. As a ranger, one of your first chores of hospitality is to cook the crew a cobbler in a Dutch oven with coals from the fire. I did carry in the mix and cans of peaches in my backpack, but the heavy Dutch ovens are stashed in wooden boxes around these first-night entry point campsites. While the crew got busy setting up camp, I would go and retrieve the Dutch oven from the box and put it near my pack. Later, I would ask one of the boys to go get it, the mix, and the cans of peaches from my pack. Incredulously, they would ask if I had packed in the Dutch oven and all this weight. We Rangers loved building the mystique of our positions, so we took every opportunity to portray ourselves as superhuman.

"Of course, I packed all of that stuff in on my back. I'm a Ranger. That's what we do!"

We were already acclimated to the altitude and didn't feel the shortness of breath that the new campers experienced. We had done most of the backcountry camp programs and had gotten pretty proficient at those skills as well.

Enjoying a delicious peach cobbler around the fire, the group began to ask questions about the black powder rifles they would be able to shoot the next day at Black Mountain. After giving them all of the true details and safety points, I told them what a crack shot I had become. "In fact," I boasted, "I can gather up all thirteen of your hats tomorrow, throw them up in the air at once, and shoot a hole through all thirteen with just a single shot!" I said this unpretentiously, with no sense of hyperbole to keep them in awe of how cool and reserved I was. There was much murmuring and then open doubt expressed by these thirteen to seventeen-year-old boys. With a shrug, I simply promised to demonstrate tomorrow when we got to Black Mountain.

We broke camp and hit the trail with great anticipation as we headed to Black Mountain. Along the trail, we made sure to point out bear scat and other animal tracks and signs. When we arrived after lunch, the boys set up camp and then rushed to the black powder rifle range. The backcountry staff who remain at the camp all summer are dressed as old miners and trappers. They gave a safety orientation and demonstration on how to fire the rifles downrange. Each boy got a chance to shoot one of the smoky rifles with its large 50 caliber ball. After they all completed their turn, the topic turned to my boast from the night before. I solemnly collected all thirteen of their hats and stacked them right on top of one another like so many pancakes. Then I matter-of-factly tossed them about six inches above the barrel of a rifle and pulled the trigger. The stack of hats flew about six feet into the air and came down in a small shower of hats to the ground. Technically true to my word, each hat had a bullet hole from the same

Black Powder Rifle Shooting at Black Mountain

singular bullet. These became favorite souvenirs for some of the boys, which they proudly wore for the rest of their trip.

That night around the campfire, the shooting story was a favorite shared experience as they all denied ever thinking that it was possible to pull off. The topic then turned to bear signs observed along the trail and the need to hang our food and other "smellables" in the bear bags at least ten feet off the ground between two trees and approximately eight feet from either trunk.

And so it went; for three days I would teach, train, and question the group while also assessing the fitness and physical health of each crew member before leaving them on the morning of the fourth day. With a three-day rotation, most of us Rangers began to lose track of what day of the week we were actually on. Each fourth morning we would radio back to base camp to learn if we had to hike back alone quickly to base camp to meet another crew or if we were getting a day off to visit our staff friends in the backcountry or hike with another Ranger who had a day off.

When we had a new crew to meet back at base camp, we hiked alone and swiftly since we were always at least two days in from hiking with our previous crew. Sometimes we would hike out to the nearest highway and try to hitchhike in. There was a regular camp called Rocky Mountain Scout Camp where leaders who were going through training at the Philmont Training Center could bring their kids under fourteen to spend a week while receiving their training. It was also a spot to place boys who were pulled off the trail for physical ability reasons or, in some cases, because their leader had lied about their age and hoped to sneak them along. This was a terrible situation for those boys. They were separated from their group and put in a camp with other boys they did not know.

One day I was hiking back in by myself to base camp, and I encountered one of these boys who had gone "over the wall," as we called it. He was running away from the Rocky Mountain Scout Camp, trudging with his head down, boot laces untied, and looking tired and thirsty. He asked if I could hike with him in the opposite direction for a while, and I said sure. He angrily told me his tale of woe, and I simply listened and agreed with his plight. I shared some water with him and then asked, "Did you bring any water with you?"

"No."

"Did you bring any food with you?"

Again, "No."

"Have you thought about how to handle a bear encounter?"

Trembling now, "No."

"Well, I'm sure you'll be fine! Here are a couple of granola bars. Good Luck!" and I turned around and headed off back toward base camp.

He lasted about one hundred yards and then came running back after me, pleading with me to take him back to Rocky Mountain Scout Camp. We hiked back in with him talking the whole way and me just listening to him. It was an epiphany moment for me. Wasn't I just like this young boy trying to run away from my problems in anger? Was God looking at me the same way I was dealing with the boy? Waiting for me to recognize my own situation instead of trying to compel me to do something I wasn't ready to do yet? Don't we all reach points like this in our journey through the wilderness when we don't understand the danger we are getting ourselves into? I was beginning to soften on this "will to obey" thing. I was out in His creation and was reminded of just how powerful and awesome He is. I was ready to hike back to base camp with Him to begin my professional career.

Mike Seipert, Jim Luebbert,
David Savage end of the trail

THE WILDERNESS CREATES
OPPORTUNITIES FOR US TO
DISCOVER THINGS ABOUT
OURSELVES. WHEN WE
ARE OUT IN CREATION, IT
HELPS US GET CLOSER
TO THE CREATOR.

THE BACHELOR WILDERNESS

When my employment at Philmont concluded in early August of 1982, I packed up the old 1964 Mercury Comet for the last time and drove home to San Angelo to purchase my very first new vehicle. It was a dark blue Toyota pickup truck. I put a superb aftermarket Alpine stereo in it so I could blast all of my favorite music as loud as I liked and sing along as I drove from San Angelo to Houston to begin my engineering career. I financed that truck at an interest rate of 18%! I also took out a personal loan of $3,500 to purchase a nice new pair of cowboy boots, lots of slacks, shirts, and ties to create a professional wardrobe—along with an expensive pair of Serengeti sunglasses. After I put down the first and last month's rent on the condo I had secured through the company locator; those funds were gone. That loan through the base Credit Union was financed at an astonishing 16% interest rate, and I made payments for 48 months to pay off the funds I'd spent in 48 hours! The high-interest notes at that time were a big lesson on credit early on.

My first brand new vehicle
1982 Toyota truck

In Harris County, full coverage on a brand-new truck versus liability only on an old Comet in Tom Green County was quite a rude awakening! I ended up paying $200 a month for insurance when I had been paying only $200 a year. This killed my cash flow and tanked my budget. I realized that I was going in the red each month and had to break the lease on the condo, forfeiting the full month's rent deposit after only five months of living in Houston. I got a small efficiency apartment and licked my financial wounds as a consequence of an early lesson from the big city wilderness in which I now was.

My employer, Turner Collie & Braden Consulting Engineers (TCB), had landed a large contract with the Harris County Flood Control District to develop new Federal Emergency Management Agency (FEMA) one-hundred-year flood insurance rate maps for the entire county. My job was to model the hydrology and hydraulics of all of the watersheds in Harris County to develop these maps. I enjoyed the work and my coworkers. I got involved in all the company-sponsored team events like bowling and flag football and made many meals out of happy hour buffets with my work friends.

I was very keen on my work to do mission and was pleased with my progress professionally. I was even looking for a church to attend and was ready to get back on track with my will to obey after my epiphany at Philmont with the "over the wall" runaway. But I still was not trusting God on the woman to love purpose. In my mind, I had concluded that all of the divorces in my family could be attributed to marriage at too young an age. Naively, I thought that living longer chronologically would somehow impart more wisdom through life experience. There were lots of beautiful ladies in Houston, Texas, so I was open to dating and companionship but still very closely guarding my heart.

I had many friends from A&M that were from Houston and working there as well. One of our little sisters in the fraternity named Sandy Castillo lived in an apartment complex near where I lived and introduced me to a group of people from her complex. Many of them were international folks and were taking English as a second language course together. I really enjoyed their company and learning about their customs, holidays, and traditions as Sandy and I taught them about being a Texan. One young lady named Helen was a red-headed French-Canadian au pair who really caught my eye. We dated for a while, but then I felt vulnerable and needed to move on for my safety. I met another attractive young lady named Wendy, who had moved down from Sandusky, Michigan, to work in the Medical Center in telemetry. We became more serious, but I again broke up without giving a very good explanation. This cycle became my pattern with female relationships.

At the same time, many of my friends were all getting married to their college sweethearts, and I attended many weddings during the first few years after college. One of my best friends and a fraternity brother, Damian Luna, and I seemed very much like Owen Wilson and Vince Vaughn in the movie "Wedding Crashers." We were actually invited to the weddings we attended, but neither of us was too serious about much of anything beyond having a great time. It was the eighties, and Reagan was president. The decade was known for "conspicuous consumption," and people our age were all trying to become "yuppies" (Young Urban Professionals). The status symbols that showed you were a success were BMW automobiles and Rolex watches. In fact, there is a great joke from that period about a particular yuppie getting in a serious automobile accident. The state trooper arrived at the scene of a totaled BMW, and the driver was hanging out the window of the driver's side, moaning in pain. When he got to the victim, the trooper heard him moaning over and over, "My beautiful Beamer, oh no, my beautiful Beamer..."

Surveying his injuries, the trooper suggested that the driver might be more concerned about the amputation of his left arm. When the driver looked down to where his arm should have been, he gasped, "Oh no! My Rolex! My Rolex!"

It's a bit over the top, but I love telling jokes and was well known for it throughout my school and scouting years. I was actually coerced by a group of girls that Damian and I ran with to do amateur night at the Comedy Workshop in downtown Houston. I did do it twice, but the audience was mean-spirited on the second try and heckled the performer before me right off the stage. What a terrifying experience! I decided to go mean first and insult certain members of the crowd, which actually got them all laughing but had me running for my life in the parking lot afterward. I could officially scratch "comedian" off of any future career moves.

I decided to find a roommate to decrease my expenses, so I got an apartment together with another recent A&M grad and good friend named Sealy Morris. Sealy was starting his own company in the drill collar business with some seed money from his dad. His company was called Prideco. If you have ever lived with someone who is "all in" starting their own business, you can appreciate the difficulty of anyone who chooses this path. Sealy would actually be running the machine himself into the wee hours of the morning and come home with burn holes in his clothes from the hot metal shavings being thrown off the lathe. When it was time to play, though, Sealy and I were equally robust on both sides of the work hard play hard equation.

I was more financially challenged than my two running buddies, so when we planned a snow ski trip together, I was going to scotch-guard waterproof a pair of jeans to wear skiing rather than buy an expensive bib. I went to a very high-end ski shop to pick up a good pair of gloves, and they had a box stuffed full of entry slips for a men's head to toe ski package drawing. I filled out my slip and crammed it into the top of the box. A few days later, I was getting dressed for work and heard my name called as the drawing winner on the local radio station hosting the contest. It included skis, boots, poles, and all of the clothing, goggles, and equipment I would ever need for snow skiing. I ended up being the best dressed on the slopes of Colorado, and we all had a fantastic time. Life was full of fun and friends.

Head to toe new ski gear
(David, Damian, Sealy L-R)

I was transferred to the Austin branch office of TCB in 1984, just as the Austin area was beginning to boom. I had also completed the big flood control project in Houston and wanted to get into more land development work. I moved to Austin and found another old fraternity brother to live with as a roommate. Perry was working on a master's degree at the University of Texas and worked in the evenings as a bartender at the La Mansion hotel. This was the premium hotel where all of the rock bands who came through Austin stayed not far from the Drum concert venue on campus. Perry got to running in a very hard-partying crowd, and I became concerned about him. We had an incident with a neighbor where he was almost shot as an intruder, and I decided it was time for an intervention. We went our separate ways, and he met a wonderful lady who later helped get him on a better path.

I was literally pinballing my way through this new bachelor wilderness through a series of short girlfriend relationships and rotating roommate situations. Everything seemed to be about getting as much playing time with each spring-loaded launch of the ball bearing. In the game, you use flippers and shove the machine to try to send the ball back up for more action. Eventually, as gravity constantly works against you, your ball falls between the flippers and out of action. It is a game. It is entertaining and exciting in the moment, but in the end, all you really did was kill time. Just like in the game itself, there were lots of bells and lights going on and off as I bounced off all of the bumpers I possibly could to score points ... and ended up just killing time.

I began attending the First United Methodist Church near the state capitol and got involved in their singles class. I joined Toastmasters to improve my public speaking skills, which were required almost every weeknight for various board and city council meetings reviewing our development projects. I even applied for a White House Fellowship in the Reagan Administration but was not selected. And lastly, I became very involved in the Austin Jaycees, a coed Junior Chamber of Commerce organization.

I met another nice young lady from South Africa who was a fellow A&M graduate and was working at Vinson and Elkins, a legal firm we did a lot of work with. Her name was Karen, and things seemed to be progressing nicely. Unfortunately, she was pretty fresh out of a divorce and got spooked before I did, so she cut off the relationship. Through all of these fits and starts in romantic relationships, I never was truly intentional about where I wanted any relationship to go. This nonchalant approach leads to passivity. You float along like a cork in a stream and allow the current to take you where it will. I had still received exactly zero advice from Dad on courtship or marriage, and my brother was no longer a good source after the infidelity that led to his divorce.

> I HAD RECEIVED EXACTLY ZERO ADVICE FROM DAD ON COURTSHIP OR MARRIAGE ...

I got another fraternity brother named Vol Montgomery to share a place to keep expenses down. Vol and I got along famously, and both of us were very involved in the Jaycees organization. At a Jaycees function in the Spring of 1986, I met another international young woman from Mexico City named Marina. Marina was attractive, foreign, and mysterious. She spoke two languages fluently and had moved to Austin from El Paso, where she was trying to get into architecture school at the University of Texas. A big Peso devaluation had depleted her savings, so she was working in real estate to rebuild her tuition funds. We seemed to really click and spent a tremendous amount of time together right away. The relationship quickly became intimate, and I gave her a key to our apartment. This was a mistake. I put the cart before the horse in the relationship, and this was not God's plan for marriage. I moved out and got a place of my own. Marina still had a small and lightly furnished apartment of her own, but one day she moved all of her things into mine without discussing it with me. This should have been a red flag, but I ignored it. Now we were living together as a result of my passivity, and more expectations were soon coming from her end.

I had been fanatical about playing in another radio station contest called the Sounds of Australia. Adelaide, Australia, was a sister city of Austin, Texas, and both states in their respective countries were celebrating their sesquicentennials. The local T.V. and radio stations had exchanged staffs to a small degree, and there was an all-expense-paid trip to Australia and a thousand-dollar gift certificate to Whole Earth Provisions up for grabs. Marina and I both ended up qualifying for the final drawing by becoming the ninth caller to identify a sound effect when they played the daily contest. These were extraordinary odds in itself as there were only a total of eighty people who could be ninth callers, so if we agreed to take one another, we had a one in forty chance of winning. They drew her name, and we were off to Australia. It was a fantastic trip, and we had extended it a week to rent a campervan and travel around the South Island of New Zealand. Prior to winning the trip, I had just left TCB for another consulting engineering firm and explained that there was a possibility of winning the trip. They said, "If you win it, we will let you have the time off."

When we came back from the trip, I was promptly laid off because the Austin boom had gone bust. My entire career focus had been to get my Professional Engineer's license, so I got a job with the Texas

Water Commission to remain in Austin and complete my P.E. application to receive my license after five years of work experience. Marina was applying steadily growing pressure on me for us to get married. I wasn't opposed to the idea completely and had even been shopping for an engagement ring, but I didn't like the way she

Cuddly Koala Bear in Cleland Conservation Park in Adelaide, Australia

was trying to drive the timetable. In my mind, I was thinking; *I'm twenty-six now. Most of my friends are married now. I am growing weary of the pinball wilderness of relationships. I guess I might as well give in.* Again, this was my failure.

I knew we had big religious differences as well as some cultural ones. We both wanted children, but we gave no thought to discussing how raising them might look. We got engaged, and I even agreed to get married in Mexico City in the Catholic church. Very few of my friends and family made the wedding, and my single most important request, to take my vows in English, was not met. On May 21, 1988, our ceremony was entirely in Spanish and mostly meaningless to me spiritually. Looking back, there had been many red flags that I had simply chosen to ignore. If we had not been living together and sexually active prior to our marriage, I might have had a more intentional approach in choosing my life mate. I had almost made it to my theoretical age twenty-eight formula, which I had calculated as the age where I believed people were more ready to be married. My problem was that I had not sought any marital advice from anyone and had not had a relationship with any woman for more than six months before meeting Marina.

I was lost in the wilderness of trying to fulfill my purpose of finding a woman to love and ended up passively settling on a comfort station rather than moving intentionally toward a defined destination of my own choosing and trying to follow God's plan for marriage.

LOOKING FOR A
FEW GOOD MEN

I got engaged and also received my Professional Engineer (P.E.) license for the state of Texas in 1987. It was a big year for me! I had at last found my woman to love, had completed a major milestone in my work to do and was doing my best to obey God's will as I comprehended it. I truly enjoyed Civil Engineering as a profession, but I noticed that my career had me moving to places that were booming like Austin when the housing and rent were high and leaving places like Houston in a down market where the housing prices were dropping. Following a bust/boom cycle selling low and buying high was a value destruction model. I was also required to attend many evening meetings and hearings to represent my land development clients, and there was no overtime or additional pay in exchange for a lot of extra hours. Lastly, there was no compensation recognition for superior performance in getting your projects through the Austin governmental bureaucracy. After leaving TCB and getting laid off at the other consulting firm in a slowing Austin market, I was having doubts about my work to do. I did not enjoy working as a bureaucrat at the Texas Water Commission in the Hazardous and Solid Waste Permitting Department, but it had gotten me through the completion of my P.E. goal.

My good friend Damian had changed jobs a year earlier and was now working for Nalco Chemical Company, the world's largest water treatment company. He said that working in technical sales was where I should be and that Nalco was always looking for good people. At that point in my life, my sales experience was fundraising events for scouts or band—peddling chocolate, wind chimes, or some other products that no one really needed or wanted. I thought of sales like car salesmen, and I didn't have a very high regard for the profession from my experience with it. But Damian pointed out that technical sales with Nalco meant I would be selling engineering and chemical application expertise to go along with the chemical products. It was a large, global company with a great compensation plan where your commission was uncapped. You also had the top benefits of a Fortune 500 corporation, a company car, and an expense account to entertain your customers hunting and fishing or going to ball games.

I read a great book at the time called *Work With Passion: How to Do What You Love For a Living* by Nancy Anderson. After carefully going through the book and completing its exercises at the end of each chapter, I concluded that technical sales were actually an extremely good fit for me. Damian got the interviews arranged, and on July 7, 1987, Marina and I moved to Corpus Christi. I began my new career with Nalco Chemical Company, selling process chemicals to the refining industry along the ship channel there. It was extremely technical work which appealed to my engineering mind, and I thoroughly enjoyed the relationship building and flexible schedule.

We bought our first home just two blocks from Corpus Christi Bay after we were married in 1988. We had only been in the house a few months when Hurricane Gilbert filled the entire Gulf of Mexico as a Category 5, and it was predicted to be a direct hit on Corpus Christi. When Sealy and I had lived together back in August of 1983, we rode out Hurricane Alicia, a Category 3 storm, in our apartment. It was a frightening experience! We had to climb out the window to get out due to tree limbs blocking our front door. Alicia caused extensive damage across the Houston area, and we had no power for a week. I couldn't imagine what Gilbert, a Category 5, would do to our home only two blocks from the Bay. The media frenzy was ridiculous as out of town news reporters poured into town to cover the destruction. Fortunately, the storm veered west into Mexico and extreme south Texas, and our home was spared.

On February 15, 1990, my life was forever changed as I became a father for the first time. Our daughter, Nicole, was scheduled to be a Valentine for us but stubbornly resisted until the following day, coming into this world at a healthy eight pounds ten ounces. Her younger brother, Dayton, was born twenty-two months later as a late Christmas present on December 27, 1991. He was the nursery champ weighing in at nine pounds five ounces. I cannot overstate how significantly life changes when you become a dad. You have participated in the miracle of creating a new life! It is the first time that I can honestly say I loved someone else more than myself. Like almost any parent, I would gladly sacrifice my own life to save my child's. Becoming a parent makes you want to be the best possible person you can be because little folks are counting on you. Marina and I were both very committed to her being a stay-at-home mom and giving our two children all the love, care, and education they needed in their formative years. We wanted them to be bilingual, so Marina spoke Spanish exclusively to them, and I spoke only English. While Dayton was still an infant, we bought a Skamper pop-up camper with a commission check and began camping as a family before he could walk.

My career at Nalco was going very well, and a door was opened to me through my scouting background as a Philmont Ranger. Two refining executives worked for Citgo Petroleum, who were old scouting people. They were looking for "a few good men," as the Marine Corps slogan goes. They wanted to get a backpacking group together and heard about me and my Philmont experience from a customer with whom I had worked closely in their organization. The two Citgo executives were Adolph Lechtenberger, the Operations Manager at the Corpus Christi Refinery, and Jim Schepens, the Vice President of Petrochemicals, out of their Houston office. These two gentlemen were much higher in the organization than I would typically make sales calls on, but they contacted me and asked if I was interested in going on a backpacking trip with them in the Weminuche Wilderness near Silverton, Colorado. I said, "Of Course!" but then I immediately called my boss to check with him to see how it would be handled from a paid time off standpoint. He asked about their positions and then said, "Certainly, you won't have to use your personal vacation time for spending a week with executives that we are begging to get just a one-hour meeting with most of the time."

I couldn't believe my good fortune! Here I was somewhat awestruck by their positions in the business world, and yet in the outdoor world, they esteemed me highly because of my Philmont Ranger experience.

We had a couple of breakfast meetings when Jim came to Corpus Christi and discussed gear like tents and stoves and went over the route Jim had come up with. Another executive named Joe Jeffords from Exxon, where Adolph had worked previously, was conscripted as our fourth man for the expedition. Joe had very little backpacking experience and borrowed a lot of his gear from Adolph and Jim as the new recruit. I was just turning thirty-one a few weeks after the trip in early September, and the other three were twelve to fourteen years older than me.

Adolph and I flew up to Durango, Colorado, from essentially sea level Corpus Christi. Joe drove up from Houston, and Jim met us there, flying in from Houston. We hit an outdoor store to buy white gas for our Coleman Peak One stoves and some other groceries to go along with the dehydrated meals Jim had already purchased for dinners. We hit the trail that afternoon with fifty-pound packs and zero time to acclimate to the higher elevation. The Vallecito Creek Trailhead elevation is 7,900 feet. We all immediately felt its effects as the trail went straight up the drainage! Joe even had a moment of hesitation when we stopped early to take a rest. He could barely breathe and expressed out loud that he wasn't sure he was going to be able to do this. We were still pretty close to his car at the trailhead, but we talked him out of any bailing out ideas. We hiked less than five miles up the reservoir drainage and camped along the creek for our first night on the trail.

WE HIT THE TRAIL THAT AFTERNOON WITH FIFTY-POUND PACKS AND ZERO TIME TO ACCLIMATE TO THE HIGHER ELEVATION.

Our planned route was to follow the Vallecito Creek drainage upstream to Hunchback Pass on the Continental Divide Trail.

Hunchback Pass elevation is 12,493 feet, an average grade of 10% over the nineteen-and-a-half-mile distance from the trailhead. The second day was more of the same, a struggle to get enough oxygen into our lungs with lots of sweating and not enough hydration in the dry mountain air. Our high salt diet of salami, cheese, and crackers for lunch was probably not the best either in retrospect. The scenery was spectacular along the creek, but we weren't on top of anything yet to capture the truly exquisite views.

As the youngster and Ranger, I was typically leading the group. We were using 1954 photo revised USGS Quad Maps and quickly learned that there were many more trails on the ground than our old maps showed. On the morning of the third day, we came to a junction in the trail where there were two well-defined paths heading off in different directions to different drainages. There was only one trail shown on the map. We paused and studied the map very carefully. I was certain of the topography, drainage, contours and other indications on the map that we should take the left or western leading trail. Adolph was equally certain that the right trail was the way to go. I was not going to argue with high-ranking clients. I respected these men and their authority and would defer to their decisions even if I was in disagreement. This is how we Rangers taught the Senior Patrol Leaders at Philmont. You let them make a mistake and hike the extra miles until they figure it out on their own. Besides, I was younger and could easily hike the extra miles.

We took the trail to the right and continued up through a bunch of thick willow shrubs to the top of a divide. It was difficult hiking at an elevation of over 10,000 feet now. We found a lake just down from the pass we had come over and sat down beside it for a snack and a packs-off break. Adolph asked to see the map, and I handed it to him. He studied it quietly for a very long time. I finally said that it didn't matter how long he looked at it; we were no longer hiking in territory that was on that map. Generally, it is not a good idea to be totally off the map, but those quad maps were at a scale that didn't cover an extremely large area. Next, there was a lot of murmuring. Jim looked at the map, and Joe was foolishly trusting the rest of us, probably regretting not choosing his bail-out option earlier. We finally came to the consensus that we were, in fact, lost and probably off of the maps we had brought with us. This is when the wilderness finds out if you compound your mistakes or take your medicine and hike back to a known and well-defined point on your map.

The moment of truth on being lost

We were in some beautiful high country above the tree line somewhere around 13,000 feet in elevation. We could see far in all directions and thought we would try to triangulate our position based upon other ranges or prominent mountains that we could see. We were trying to get to Hunchback Pass to get on our correct, planned route. We decided that we could bushwhack through the scrubby willow all around us and across a snow chute to the next drainage over. This was a doubling down of our initial error. Hiking in high country off the trail is never a great idea unless you really know the country, but we were stubborn and didn't want to backtrack down the trail we had come up and give up all that elevation. Between the exertion, elevation, and most likely a little dehydration, Adolph and Joe were feeling altitude sickness symptoms. We scraped our way through the brush and spooked up a huge mule deer, and even found an arrow from a recent elk hunter's errant shot. Oh yeah, that's another good reason not to be bushwhacking up here at this time of year—it was bow season for elk hunting! We figured many of the unmapped trails led to hunting camps that had been well established by guides in the area.

We made it over to the other drainage divide and looked down a huge glacial U-shaped valley, which we believed was Ute Gulch, and saw a herd of about fifty elk. Now *that* was a payoff for the exertion in my book. Not many people get up there to see a whole herd in the wild in their high-country habitat. We were all wiped out, so we found a spot to camp below the pass. Adolph had gotten quite nauseous and could only get a Cup-o-Soup down for dinner. Joe was not in very good shape either. I was beginning to wonder if I would be part of some terrible experience that these guys, my customers, were never going to forget. Jim and I were tentmates, so we got out our candle lantern and began to study the map in earnest. Then the rain began.

The next morning, we were shrouded in fog and drizzle. Our visibility was horrible, and we had counted on being able to see clearly to confirm our map reading interpretation from the previous night. Now our tents and other gear were wet and heavier. I went back up

Recalculating ... I believe this was Ute Gulch

to the top to reconnoiter and heard the elk bugling in the distance, seeming to mock our misfortune. I figured out where we were by finding a sign. We were in Starvation Gulch well north and east of Hunchback Pass. Ominously, I also found an elk skeleton in Starvation Gulch, and things were beginning to feel a bit grim. I knew we had to get back on our map and chart a route on a trail that would get us there. Adolph was getting worse, and we were all growing concerned. He threw up and began showing worse altitude sickness symptoms, heading toward Acute Mountain Sickness, which is quite serious. He said he thought he could hike if I could take some of his weight off him. I took his tent and put my pack weight north of 60 pounds, which was wearing me out fast. It was drizzling and raining, and now we were beginning to worry about hypothermia as well.

We found a good trail and I was confident we were heading back in the right direction to Hunchback Pass and out to Elk Park along the Silverton Railroad, our planned exit point from the wilderness. Adolph was still getting sick and I could not carry any additional weight. At this point, we all became equals in the wilderness. Adolph's pride was wounded, and he was trying to insist that he could get himself out. I pulled out my Ranger Field Book and showed him the First Aid section covering altitude sickness combined with hypothermia leading to Acute Mountain Sickness. It said in black and white that the symptoms could progress to death. It was time to make a decision. Joe was barely any better than Adolph, so Jim and I said that we would offload our pack weight as much as possible, leaving them with all the food and fuel. We would then hike eighteen miles all the way out to Elk Park that afternoon and try to catch the first train coming up the narrow-gauge railroad in the morning from Durango to Silverton. Once in Silverton, we would get in touch with the Sheriff and EMT folks to get a four-wheel-drive to come up the old mining road to rescue Joe and Adolph. Joe and Adolph needed to get in their tent, in their sleeping bags, and keep warm and dry in the rain until we could get back with help.

On our rapid hike out, Jim kept talking about a four-star dude ranch that he had read about in some American Express literature he received that was located near the Elk Park Trailhead. We would try to find it and stay there the night to get help on the way more quickly. It was the only thing that kept us going through a grueling eighteen-mile hike in the rain through rugged country. We finally got to the railroad stop, and there was no dude ranch. We each hiked an additional mile in both directions to search and then came back to setup a cold camp without food in the rain. I was fuming at Jim for building up false hopes of comfort that were mere fantasy, but I was more worried about Adolph and Joe back up in the mountains.

Early in the morning, one of those two-person cars came along the track doing an inspection for rockfall before the train came. We stopped them and told them about our emergency, so one of them got off, and Jim went up to Silverton with the other man to summon the sheriff and an EMT. I caught the train itself an hour later. A large group of Amish or Mennonite people were on the train; most were women in their long print dresses and bonnets. I was quite ripe smelling and pretty filthy, so no one wanted me to sit next to them. I finally sat down next to one of the men and silently looked out the window, wondering how Jim was doing with the rescue folks.

Two four-inch logs across the channel rolled and caused a spill, nearly headlong into the creek!

Jim went with the sheriff and an EMT in the 4WD vehicle to be sure they could find where we left Adolph and Joe. I later learned that Adolph's blood pressure was extremely high, at stroke levels, when they got to him, but he responded quickly to oxygen to bring it down. In fact, it was amazing to see how quickly he recovered once we got fluids in him and got him down to lower elevations. We had narrowly escaped a real tragedy and had learned a lot in the process. After some time in the local hospital to fully check all of Adolph's vitals and hydration level, we were pressed to find a ride back to Durango in time to make our flights home. We found a good Samaritan woman with a son who needed to see a doctor in Durango, and she agreed to haul us and our gear down to Durango with them.

I had found a few good men, and they had found me. After a dubious beginning to our backpacking adventures, we decided to do it again the next year with a ceiling of 10,000 feet for the maximum elevation. Adolph and Jim would become lifelong friends and advisors who taught me more about the industry around our campfires than I would ever learn in any training manuals.

Edwin Markham said, "There is a destiny which makes us brothers; none goes his way alone. All that we send into the lives of others comes back into our own." Life is not meant to be lived alone—we were meant to traverse together. "Two heads are better than one," is how Solomon put it. I have learned the value of developing and maintaining meaningful relationships with other men. The benefits are multiplied when men venture into nature together, free from cell phones and pavement, calendar requests, and the good guest towels. Under the wide-open sky, connection comes naturally. Iron sharpens iron as wisdom and experience are exchanged in profound ways. And when you find yourself in life's wilderness— totally off the map and in distress—there is nothing more priceless than trusted, worthy companions who will help you back to safety and then take up the trail with you once again.

> LIFE IS NOT MEANT TO BE LIVED ALONE— WE WERE MEANT TO TRAVERSE TOGETHER.

CHAPTER ELEVEN

CLEANING THINGS UP

Becoming a father had significantly motivated me to become the best person I could be. After the failure of the other marriages in my family and seeing the wreckage of divorce manifested in the lives of the innocent children involved, I was determined to make my marriage work and be the very best husband and father I could be. I knew that this would require some changes in old selfish patterns of behavior and thought, where I had been living more according to my own will than to God's will. I was intentional and sincere about my surrender. Once we moved to Corpus Christi, the first step was finding a church and getting our children baptized and dedicated to the Lord right from the beginning. I was raised in the Methodist

Nicole and Dayton Christmas 1994

faith and much more committed to church than Marina, so we joined First United Methodist Church (FUMC) on the Bay a few short miles from our home.

My mother was always the dominant force when it came to faith in our family, and she was indeed a fierce warrior for the Lord. I think much of this was due to her experience as a military wife, which required strength and independence in so many situations when my father was not around. She modeled a strong Christian walk and was relentless throughout her life in encouraging her children to do the same.

I'm not sure of the date, but she had been on a spiritual retreat called a Walk to Emmaus sometime right after our kids were born. She claimed it was an extraordinary experience for her and talked about it often in 1993 and 1994. She insisted that I needed to go on the same retreat and even offered to pay for it. When I asked her more about it, she said that it was a three-day weekend retreat where they take your watch away and didn't offer many more details. I didn't like the vague answers and lack of details. It felt cultish to me and raised suspicion. She resumed her campaign of insistence and told me that the only reason she would not share more was that it would ruin some of the delightful surprises in store. Well, if you can't trust your mom, who can you trust? FUMC had an established Emmaus Community as it was called, and I had heard positive things about it from others I trusted in my local church. I signed up for Walk Number 364 to be conducted at Bishop Drury Retreat Center right there in Corpus on June 16-19, 1994.

We participants, called pilgrims, checked in and surrendered our watches on a Thursday night. The retreats are either all male or all female, so it was kind of like checking into a men's locker room atmosphere where none of us knew exactly what to expect. I knew many of the other pilgrims. In fact, one was another good friend and old fraternity brother named Jim Pickett. The Spiritual Director was our pastor, Mark Doty, and the lay director, Wayne Kelly, was also from our church. There were snacks, soft drinks, and a good-natured kidding atmosphere to help put everyone at ease about the uncertain agenda ahead for the long weekend. They had us all do an ice breaker exercise to get to know the person next to us and then had everyone introduce "My New Best Friend" to the larger group, seventy-five in total. Then they had a wide-open Q&A session asking everyone to speak about their thoughts on the retreat, how they ended up there, and to express any apprehensions. As others began to humorously share their concerns about the cult feel, some of the staff folks I knew began teasing one another about their first experiences as pilgrims. Without really thinking it through, I decided to tell a joke that seemed just perfect for the situation—as I so often did. This particular joke could be introduced without anyone knowing it was a joke. I raised my hand and was called on to share. I began:

"I was kind of anxious about the lack of an agenda and taking the watches away, to be honest. In fact, I had a really peculiar dream last night. I dreamt that many of us here had all died somehow at the same time, and that we all ended up in hell together! Satan was standing in front of a wall full of clocks with all our names on them, and the hands were all moving around the faces at different speeds, some quite fast and others quite slowly. I asked Satan, 'What do these clocks represent?' He said, 'They represent the amount of time each of you spent masturbating during your time on earth.'"

I must pause here to interject that this brought Coke-through-the-nose laughter from many other pilgrims, especially my good friend Jim who couldn't believe I was telling this at a church retreat!

Once I had begun, I realized this was probably a huge blunder, but I was too far gone to stop.

"Well, Satan, I see my own clock and others here all seem to have one, but one person's is missing?"

I knew Jim's brother-in-law well. He was an attorney and staff volunteer, and he had just zinged another guy pretty good, so I chose him as the butt of the joke.

"Satan, where is Charles' clock?"

Satan replied, "Oh, his is on the ceiling! We're using it for a fan!"

The eruption of laugher rolled across the entire group and did take a great deal of tension out of the room. Charles got a little red-faced, but I knew he would be okay. Just as the room began to settle again, the laughter would erupt again. No one could believe what I had done, and suddenly everyone felt much more spiritual than me.

Mark Doty, our pastor, finally looked at me and said, "Gee David, no one has ever been kicked off a Walk to Emmaus before! You could be the first!"

Then he went on to make jokes of his own, "It really is a sticky subject. Beats me why?"

He then transitioned into a more serious tone. He segued to the subject of pornography, talking about its negative effects on marriages and emphasizing that it was a huge concern of the church. He went on to say that lust of the eyes was a sin that all men struggle with—especially since the sexual revolution of the seventies and women dressing more provocatively every day, even in church. I think all of the men in the room were now more comfortable and were ready to have an incredible experience because our pastor was being transparent, honest, and genuine about his own weakness in the flesh.

The Walk to Emmaus retreat did have several very special surprises that made it one of the true mountaintop experiences of my life, both spiritually and in feeling God's love for me. It is not my place to reveal those special surprises here because some of my readers may want to experience those for themselves. I can tell you that the goal of the retreat is to help pilgrims experience God's agape love for an uninterrupted seventy-two-hour period. The definition of *agape* given in Webster's Dictionary is:

1. The love of God or Christ for humankind.

2. The love of Christians for other persons corresponding to the love of God for humankind.

3. Unselfish love of one person for another without sexual implications; brotherly love.

The goal was achieved on my Walk, and I went on to serve on the staff of another one to watch its effect on other men. Transformational is the best word I can use to describe the experience.

Of course, once the retreat was over, we all had to return to the world as it was. It reminds me of the first golf lesson I ever had. The instructor watched me hit a dozen or more balls and evaluated my swing mechanics. He pointed out some easy-to-fix aspects like my grip, address to the ball, and alignment toward the target. I was amazed at the improved accuracy and distance with just those few adjustments right there in the first lesson. Then he told me to go to the range and hit about a thousand balls over the next few weeks to build muscle memory and consistency before I could return for another lesson. We all know that the key to excellence is in the discipline of practice. Suppose a person is trying to clean up his sinful nature. He first has to understand and accept it intellectually and then become more aware of the situations where he is most vulnerable. We all have different strengths and weaknesses. I believe that the weakness of the flesh is common to all of us. I found a terrific resource on this topic: the appropriately named book, *Every Man's Battle: Every Man's Guide to Winning the War on Sexual Temptation One Victory at a Time*. The coauthors Stephen Arterburn and Fred Stoeker do an excellent job on this topic. My favorite metaphor in the book is described in the excerpt below:

> *Let's expand a bit on this metaphor to help you better understand our goal of reining in our roving minds.*
>
> *Once, you were a proud mustang, wild and free. Sleek and rippling, you ranged the hills and valleys, running and mating where you willed, master of your destiny. God, owner of a large local ranch, noticed you from a distance as He worked His herd. Though you took no notice of Him, He loved you and desired to make you His own. He sought you in many ways, but you ran from him again and again.*
>
> *One day He found you trapped in a deep, dark canyon, with no way out. With the lariat of salvation, He gently drew you near, and you became one of His own. He desired to break you, that you might be useful to Him and bring Him further joy. But knowing your natural ways and how you loved to run free*

with the mares, He set a fence around you. This corral was the perimeter of the eyes. It stopped the running and kept you from sniffing the winds and running wildly over the horizon.

While the corral stopped the running, it hasn't yet stopped the mating. You mate in your mind, through attractions, thoughts, and fantasy, flirting and neighing lustily at the mares inside or near your corral. You must be broken.

I just love the visual imagery in this metaphor and think that maybe others can identify with the concept as well. It reminds me of the instinct versus intellect struggle that I mentioned in chapter six. The question is this: "How do we get the practice in reining in our roving minds?"

The Walk to Emmaus placed a strong emphasis on small group fellowship through weekly reunion group meetings. Every meeting had an order of the reunion. The three key components were:

1. Closest to Christ – At what moment during the past week did you feel closest to Christ?

2. Call to Discipleship – At what moment during the past week did you feel you were responding to God's call to be His disciple?

3. Discipleship Denied – When was your faith tested this week through failure?

Meeting weekly in a safe environment with other men you trust and confessing where your discipleship was denied is how to get that practice. In my reunion group, we talked about losing our tempers, reining in our roving minds, and struggling with foul language, as a few examples.

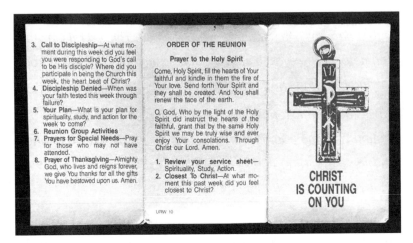

3. **Call to Discipleship**—At what moment during this week did you feel you were responding to God's call to be His disciple? Where did you participate in being the Church this week, the heart beat of Christ?
4. **Discipleship Denied**—When was your faith tested this week through failure?
5. **Your Plan**—What is your plan for spirituality, study, and action for the week to come?
6. **Reunion Group Activities**
7. **Prayers for Special Needs**—Pray for those who may not have attended.
8. **Prayer of Thanksgiving**—Almighty God, who lives and reigns forever, we give You thanks for all the gifts You have bestowed upon us. Amen.

ORDER OF THE REUNION

Prayer to the Holy Spirit

Come, Holy Spirit, fill the hearts of Your faithful and kindle in them the fire of Your love. Send forth Your Spirit and they shall be created. And You shall renew the face of the earth.

O, God, Who by the light of the Holy Spirit did instruct the hearts of the faithful, grant that by the same Holy Spirit we may be truly wise and ever enjoy Your consolations. Through Christ our Lord. Amen.

1. **Review your service sheet**—Spirituality, Study, Action.
2. **Closest To Christ**—At what moment this past week did you feel closest to Christ?

URW 10

CHRIST IS COUNTING ON YOU

The point is that you cannot hold yourself accountable with self-talk. If you honestly want to clean things up to become the best father and husband you can be, you are going to have to tell another person that you want to do that and ask them to hold you accountable to the standard you have provided. Then, to build your "muscle memory" or new thought patterns, you will have to practice a great deal to create new and healthier habits. Additionally, you will need to confess when you have failed to another person so that you have help in holding yourself accountable.

When you go backpacking in the wilderness for a week, you get quite dirty. You sweat a lot, so you begin to stink. Your hands are dirty from building fires and pitching tents in the dirt. You can ignore it for a day or two, but by the third day, the funk in your sleeping bag becomes unbearable. Your clammy legs stick together in your mummy bag, and your oily scalp begins to stain your pillow. You become aware that you may even be impacting your tentmate in such close personal space. And let's not get into too much detail on how feet and socks begin to smell. It is the same with sinful behavior. You know you are dirty, and you stink. You might even become aware that others are beginning to notice. You need to get cleaned up. On our backpacking adventures, our little group can't make it much past day three before we are ready to do what most people would consider insane. We are ready to strip down and dive into a mountain lake that might have been snow just a few days before. Slowly wading in just can't be done. It is simply too cold and breathtaking to do that. It has to be a full commitment plunge, completely immersive! At times, I have honestly thought I could walk on water to get out of that icy grip. Your lungs burn. There is no way to take a deep breath. Extremities shrink, and every pore of your skin slams shut. You try to take it for as long as you can while you scrub the dirt off of your head, face, arms, and legs. Then you sprint like Michael Phelps for the shore and your tiny backpacking towel. You can't feel your ears at first, but slowly, the circulation returns to your limbs. As you finish drying off and look for a rock to stretch out on in the sun like a prehistoric lizard, your tingling body has never felt cleaner. What a truly glorious feeling it is to become clean!

Taking the cold plunge in the Sawtooth
Wilderness with Joe and Adolph

A desire to be the best father I could motivated me to clean things up. I invite you to take a cleansing plunge today. Recognize areas where you struggle and make a commitment to become the best man you can be. Find someone you trust to share your decision with and hold you accountable to the process. There is no greater feeling than coming clean and basking in the glorious presence of the Creator. No guilt. No condemnation. No shame. Just the joyous realization that His love has covered your sins and His desire to be reconciled to you is more powerful than your desire to run from Him. Today is a good day to turn around. Take that plunge. You will not regret it.

CHAPTER TWELVE

CHEERFUL COMPANIONS

Adolph, Joe, Jim, and I had enjoyed our little backpacking quartet. After the severe altitude sickness that led to a mountain rescue for half of our crew on year one, a person might conclude that interest in subsequent adventures would wane. Rather astonishingly, this was not the case. The next year, in 1992, we doubled the size of our crew from four to eight. We did, however, set a limit on our maximum elevation. We decided we would not venture above 10,000 feet. That year we went to the Absaroka-Beartooth Wilderness in southern Montana, not far from Yellowstone National Park. That trip ended up being another harrowing survival story due to two very unusual heavy snowfall events around Labor Day that year. One of the new recruits, John Stacy, a Human Resources executive for Citgo, wrote a thirty-page short story on that trip and titled it "The Otter Lake Odyssey." I will not cover it in detail here besides mentioning that we had another lost experience due to difficulty finding the trail in deep snow and poor visibility conditions. That trip was Joe Jeffords last. One of the other recruits, a Citgo headquarters marketing executive, also decided that this, his first backpacking adventure, was enough to last him a lifetime. We added Mike Nash, an Environmental Manager for Koch Industries, and Joe Christo, an IBM sales professional who went to the same church as Adolph in Corpus Christi. These three newcomers, along with Adolph Lechtenberger, Jim Schepens, and me, came up with a name for the group, affectionately calling ourselves "The Sixpack." We faithfully planned and participated in adventures around Labor Day every year from 1991 through 2009 despite our dubious beginnings.

The Sixpack: Mike, John, Adolph, David, Joe, & Jim

Throughout this eighteen-year period, we relentlessly needled one another, laughed, fished, played cards, and shared our innermost selves around our campfires. Time spent with this band of brothers, along with my weekly Emmaus reunion group meetings, was the accountability I needed. Having these kinds of relationships with other men, many of them older and wiser than me, has been invaluable to both my personal and professional growth. It was the cheerful camaraderie and fellowship in the great outdoors that brought us back together year after year. Getting lost, bickering about map reading interpretations, hail, fires, insects, and the other unpredictable factors of being out in the elements paled in comparison to the joy of brotherhood in the wild.

Three of us were avid fishermen and insisted that every prospective trip have some good lakes or streams that provided excellent fishing opportunities. Adolph, Joe, and I were the fishermen. Jim, John, and Mike were more into day hikes to get on top of a nearby peak without a backpack on our layover day. Besides remaining at or below 10,000 feet of elevation, our criteria for each trip was a loop hike, so we weren't doubling back through country we had already seen. Preferably this was a layover day to camp in the same spot for two nights once we got back into the woods and away from the Labor Day weekend crowds who were not camping overnight. We wanted good fishing opportunities and beautiful scenery. The Sixpack backpacked in the following wilderness areas:

- Kootenay National Park in the Canadian Rockies
- The Wind River Range and Popo Agie Wilderness in Wyoming
- The Oberland Trail in Switzerland
- Kachemak Bay in Alaska
- The Sawtooths, Seven Devils, and White Cloud Peaks in Idaho

- The Absaroka Beartooth, Anaconda Pintler, Scapegoat, and Jim Bridger in Montana
- Glacier National Park in Montana
- The High Uintas in Utah

We took one canoe expedition along the Buffalo River in Arkansas. Some areas were repeated but on different trails. All in all, it was an incredible record of the spectacular beauty found only in nature's raw backcountry and seen by only those willing to do so on foot.

In his book titled *Whispers in the Wilderness*, professional landscape photographer Erik Stensland uses short reflections on nature paired with gorgeous photographs to remind us of wisdom that our busy world has forgotten. His first entry is called "Wild Embrace." See if his words don't resonate with you as profoundly as they did with me:

Above me clouds gently float past, leisurely crossing over the mountaintops without seeming to notice them. Down below me there is a large forested valley, free of trail or any obvious sign of human touch. I'm finally all alone, embraced by this mountain wilderness. As my cares fade and my body relaxes, I realize within me a deep sense of belonging. In my bones I can feel this is where I belong, or at least where I long to be.

How can this place, in some ways so inhospitable to people, seem to speak words of belonging to my deepest self? Have we cut ourselves off from the world to which we truly belong? Is the wilderness reminding me of some prehistoric relationship between humanity and nature, or is it the silence of this place that is inviting me to reunite with my inner self and with the whisper on the wind? Perhaps it is both of these and more. In this solitary place I can almost hear the wilderness whispering to each of us to come and be reconnected with nature and ourselves.

It was the stripping away of technology, the constant blitz of news and information, and the busyness of work and life demands that beckoned us back each year for our week of therapy. We could make plans, but in the end, we were always forced to adapt to what nature gave us. Furthermore, it demanded our full attention and skills to make it through all the unpredictable situations and weather unscathed for eighteen years.

One unsurprising aspect about our group of mostly type-A personalities was a strong competitive drive about almost everything— but especially fishing bragging rights and playing Hearts. I'm not sure where it originated exactly, but every time any of us were around a lake fishing and got a fish on the line, we would shout, "FIRE IN THE HOLE!" so the others would know we were catching fish and possibly moving ahead in the catch count. Not every fish was landed, and we often were catching and releasing the fish, so there was considerable opportunity for exaggeration of both the size and count of the fish. Cell phone cameras were not invented yet for most of these years, so photographic evidence was also difficult since we generally were not near one another and had our hands full landing and quickly releasing the fish. There were several trips where we caught many small brook trout but never landed any sizable fish. On other trips, we kept our catch and ate them but carrying the weight

IT WAS THE STRIPPING AWAY OF TECHNOLOGY, THE CONSTANT BLITZ OF NEWS AND INFORMATION, AND THE BUSYNESS OF WORK AND LIFE DEMANDS THAT BECKONED US BACK EACH YEAR FOR OUR WEEK OF THERAPY.

of lemons and cooking oil in addition to the frying pan eliminated this practice in the latter years when we all were trying to get our pack weights down as much as possible.

All three of us caught some sizable trout over all the years on very light tackle and four-pound test line, which makes a fish feel much larger in the moment. On some trips, we caught lots of cutthroats. Occasionally, we even caught the rare Dolly Varden or Golden trout species, but most of the time, it was Rainbows or Brookies. The high-altitude lakes we were fishing would typically freeze over in the winters and, most of the time, could not sustain a larger fish through several years of life. Through all of those cries of "Fire in the Hole," the lies about who really caught the biggest fish over all those years has never

really been settled until now. "Ole Snort," as the mythical trophy in the old Snuffy Smith comic strip was known, was landed in the White Clouds Wilderness of Idaho. I submit photographic evidence below as proof!

I know that this revelation will crush Joe and Adolph, but they will have to write their own memoirs and provide their own photographic verification to make any case otherwise!

When it came to playing Hearts, everyone was in, and

The Biggest Catch!

the competition was fierce. The number of individual mind games and strategies working with this highly intelligent group of men was numerous. If you are unfamiliar with Hearts as a card game, let me briefly outline a few of the rules. A deck of cards is shuffled, and eight cards are dealt to each of six players with the four remaining cards held blind, face down in the "kitty." After everyone examines their cards and determines a strategy for that hand, each player must pass three cards, first to his right, then left, then across, and on the fourth hand, it is a hold em'. Hearts are a trump suit taking any hand when played unless a higher heart is played on top of it. The idea is NOT to take any hands. The player with the lowest score on the scorepad after someone else goes over 100 is declared the winner. There is an opportunity to attempt to take all scoring hands in what is called a "run." If successful, the person who runs it gets zero points, and everyone else is penalized with 26 points.

Mike Nash was the most experienced Hearts player. He played year-round, while most of the rest of us only played Hearts on this trip one week a year. One might think that would give him an advantage. You would be wrong. You see, Mike thought that all of us would play what he called "ethical Hearts." Ethical Hearts assumes that everyone is equally motivated to keep the person leading on the scorepad in check and play somewhat predictably in your own self-interest to win. What is most sacrosanct is the protocol in passing your three hand-off cards. You should never pass three high cards to guard against the person you are passing to from attempting a run. You must always "hold a stopper" in ethical Hearts. That is to keep a higher card than one that you pass, so you can stop someone from running. We delighted in being contrarians to Mike's expected behaviors because this gave us the reaction from Mike, and the others we wished to entertain ourselves with, regardless of where we sat on the scorepad.

The funniest thing is that we all could count on Mike to behave in the most predictable way. When passing to others besides Mike, it became a psychological study of tendencies to try to read their patterns of behavior. Of course, at different times, different people would behave like suicide bombers just to throw people off their patterns.

Adolph was probably the most successful in running because he was also the most competitive and shrewd in discerning others' patterns who cared less about winning. We would constantly play once our camp chores were done, after meals, at lunch along the trail, and at the hotels where we stayed going to and coming off the trail. The delight we all took from playing this game was unique to each individual, but I would have to say the biggest groans and laughs always came when Mike would have kept the stopper and no one else did. He was always on the horns of a dilemma. He could stop a run, which would negatively impact him alone at something less than twenty-six points. Or he could duck the trick and shirk his responsibility to "ethical Hearts." This would assure the runner was successful, and everyone, except the runner, would be penalized with the larger twenty-six-point hit. It seemed to me this situation was a microcosm of our society. Should a person do the right thing in a given situation, which requires courage and sacrifice, or should that person duck responsibility and let everyone suffer the penalties for no one stopping the bully in a given situation? It is an interesting illustration about consequences in group dynamics.

Fishing and card-playing made every trip cheerful with competitive camaraderie and laughter. There is good reason why they say, "laughter is the best medicine." It lifts the heart, feeds the soul, and soothes the mind. In a world growing ever politically correct and more easily offendable, keeping your sense of humor is a healthy defense against the madness. Our culture esteems the workaholic. We idolize those who keep an insane pace for high achievement as they climb the ladder of success, often neglecting their families and abandoning genuine friendships. Men need to take time out to play and rest. We need to laugh until it hurts, compete, high-five, and enjoy the company of those who "get us" and simply enjoy being together. It's important.

A high-spirited hearts game in the wilderness

MEN NEED TO TAKE TIME OUT
TO PLAY AND REST. WE NEED
TO LAUGH UNTIL IT HURTS,
COMPETE, HIGH-FIVE, AND
ENJOY THE COMPANY OF THOSE
WHO "GET US" AND SIMPLY
ENJOY BEING TOGETHER.

CHAPTER THIRTEEN

SURVIVING THE AMBUSH

In my estimation, the early nineties were good years for living out my three primary purposes. I was married to a woman I loved. We both adored our children and having a family. I was actively involved in my church at FUMC in Corpus Christi and committed to my Emmaus Reunion Group, where I was held accountable to higher standards of conduct and obedience to God's will. Since joining Nalco in 1987, I was also successful in my work to do. I was making significant commissions on the bonus plan, which exceeded more than fifty percent of my total compensation, and I was nominated for Salesman of the Year in 1992. I was promoted rapidly through the field sales positions, and in 1995, I was promoted to the District Sales Manager position out of Beaumont, Texas. At the time, Marina was eager to get out of Corpus Christi and closer to a major city like Houston. Beaumont was just an hour away and seemed to meet her criteria.

There was a large adjustment for me professionally to go from superstar player to coach in a sales organization. The circumstances which led to my promotion were also unusual. The previous District Manager's wife had been diagnosed with cervical cancer and had a poor prognosis. He had four kids and went ghost on the job, neglecting almost every aspect of the position without asking for help. His employees were leaderless and were beginning to leave the company, and we were also losing business to our competitors. Of course, many of these details were left out when they were trying to convince me to accept the position. I had a geography that covered what we called the "Ark-La-Tex," a good portion of East Texas, much of Louisiana, and southern Arkansas. Accepting the job required immediate overnight travel to assess each of the salespeople in the district and the health of our business with their customers. We bought a nice home in a great neighborhood in Beaumont, but I was traveling quite a bit trying to salvage a sinking district across the full geography. I made less money for the first few years in my higher position as a manager than I had been making as a successful salesman in Corpus. Increased responsibility, less pay, and more time away traveling meant that Marina was less than excited about the new position. She was also finding Beaumont to be much more bucolic culturally than Corpus. Once Nicole and Dayton were both in school for most of the day, she became restless about what to do with herself.

By 1998 I had finally turned things around. I had totally retooled the district replacing everyone except for two people and my secretary. We solidified our major accounts in long-term contracts with good margins and had our competitors on the run in the Golden Triangle, where some of the largest refineries in the country were located. I had done a lot of planting, weeding, and watering and was certain of a large harvest of new business in the coming two years. Marina often commented that it was time to leave Beaumont, but we had agreed upon a five-year plan, and the kids were happy in their elementary school. I told her we needed to sit tight and see our plan through. Opportunities were already being discussed about higher promotions to national level positions, but these would mean significantly more travel and even less time at home with the kids. Besides that, I reminded her that we had learned the company was not always upfront about new assignments' downside aspects, just like the Beaumont promotion.

In June of 1999, I received a distressing call from my father stating that he was put in the hospital by my sister Kathy and they were keeping him there against his wishes. He asked me to come to San Angelo to help him. I dropped everything and left the following day. I learned from Kathy that she and Terry had found dad on the floor in his home after some kind of diabetic episode. He appeared to have been down for almost 48 hours and was in pretty bad shape. Besides erratic blood sugar levels, he was also very confused, and she suspected that he might have had a small stroke.

Both of my sisters worked in the medical field, so I deferred to their opinions on such matters but wondered why they needed to keep him in the hospital after he had been stabilized. He was a heavy smoker and was becoming extremely irritable about not being able to smoke and not being told why he needed to remain in the hospital. They wanted to do a sleep study on him and evaluate him for sleep apnea, but the doctor who did such studies in West Texas traveled across the area and was only in town on certain days of the week. His insurance was excellent, and it appeared to me that they just wanted to run the meter on him. I demanded that they release him to me immediately and explained that I would care for him at his home and bring him back later after they had the sleep study scheduled.

Before I got him home, I got into the house and saw what terrible shape it was in. There were cigarette burns all over the furniture and rug, including burn holes in most of his clothes. Apparently, he was falling asleep while smoking and had been effective at keeping my sisters from ever going in the house. There were spills he had only dropped paper towels on and rodent droppings all over the kitchen. I couldn't believe my father had been living like this! It was time to have an intervention with him.

I got him home and asked him about the state of the house. I asked him if he wanted to die. I knew he had been frightened badly by the diabetic episode and being off his blood pressure medication while he was down. I told him that he could no longer live by himself because his diabetes required healthy meals and close monitoring of his blood sugar. We went and looked at

I would do anything for my dad!

assisted living places, and I did the sales job of my life to convince him how good it would be. He was embarrassed about his furniture and holey clothing. I had already gone through all of his banking books and showed him that he had plenty of money. We went shopping for new clothes, a lift chair, and other new furniture. We moved him in right away. I had to sell the house and everything in it in the ten-day period I was in San Angelo. It was a massive undertaking, and I'm not sure how my sisters and I pulled it off but for the grace of God.

While all of this was happening, Marina and the kids were at a family gathering at Lake of the Ozarks. My boss also contacted me to tell me that our company had been sold to a French conglomerate called Suez and that my stock options would all become immediately vested for a nice six-figure payday. I gave the news to Marina on the phone while I was still in San Angelo to try to cheer her up because she was mad at me for not making her family reunion.

After we both got back to Beaumont a few weeks later, she asked me to meet her at a Denny's restaurant near my office for a brunch appointment. When I sat down with her, a process server stepped up and immediately handed me divorce papers. She announced that this was all already done—*fait accompli*. I have never been more shocked in my life! It was a complete and calculated ambush. She had frozen all of our financial accounts along with many other onerous temporary orders. There had been no huge fights, no warnings of this level of rift whatsoever. And worse yet, there had been no attempt to work out any problems with counseling or make any effort to try to save the marriage for our kids' sake. No, this was a rake of the table like a casino employee working a crap table. To me, it felt like an utter betrayal not only by my wife but also her entire family, as this must have been schemed collaboratively when they were all together at their reunion. Anger seethed in me like a boiling volcano. I was still very worried about my dad and his situation, and this felt like kicking a man while he was down. My emotions ping-ponged between anger and deep depression. I was devoted to my children, and now I would no longer be living with them. I thought dark, terrible thoughts. If you've been through a divorce, you will recognize these horrible feelings.

I immediately got an apartment and was sleeping on the floor with my backpacking sleeping pad and sleeping bag. I could not spend any money because it was all frozen. My married friends were still my friends, but the wives did not want their husbands spending any time with me. I became an outcast and found myself in a new and very lonely wilderness.

That year the Sixpack had planned our trip over Labor Day to Kachemak Bay Alaska, and I had been looking forward with great anticipation to visiting this state known as the last frontier. This was to be our ninth trip together for the founders and seventh for the others, so we had become quite familiar with one another by this time. I called Jim and Adolph and said I wasn't going to be able to make the trip. They would not let me back out. I was ashamed and didn't want to be around people admitting to the failure of my marriage like the rest of my family. But it was this group and being out in the real wilderness that I truly needed most. I needed the big picture perspective that puts life events in context, not only for your lifetime but for eternity. It helps to look out across a mountain range and realize how small you are. Your problems seem smaller as a result.

Imagine, if you will, having a family where you are the youngest son, and you have the good fortune of having five big brothers. That is what the Sixpack had become to me over the years. Each member of the group had helped me understand things like environmental issues across the downstream industry, human resource perspectives on handling personnel issues, insights on the performance review and promotion process, and especially varying perspectives on the big issues of the day for our nation and world. On this trip to Alaska, it became even more personal. These men carried me through my grief and pain and simply listened as I poured it out before them over the trip. When I did ask for their advice or thoughts about how to proceed, each one was extremely helpful, offering wisdom from their own experiences. I was hurting, but I was not alone.

The Alaska trip was unlike any other. You know you are really out there when you are dropped off by a boat on a beach and have to learn about tide tables to figure out when it is possible to get a boat in again. We hadn't hiked two hundred yards before encountering our first fresh pile of bear scat. We reached a roaring river and had to pull ourselves across on an ingenious two-man cable car system to reach the other side. The land was raw and wild with a plant called devil's club, which had big spines along the stalks and on the underside of its broad leaves, growing everywhere. We had a few stumbles, and that stuff would cut you up quick. But the one thing we knew we would have to deal with in unprecedented numbers were mosquitoes and biting flies.

In the hand-pulled cable car with Joe—No looking back!

Unless you have been to Alaska, there is no way to comprehend the scale of this issue. I was pumping water near a creek and was absolutely swarmed by both mosquitoes and black flies. I had a notebook I was journaling in with me and swatted my calf. I counted twenty dead in one swat! When we stopped for lunch, we had trouble eating our food without inhaling several insects with every bite. They were relentless, abundant in prolific numbers, and draining our bodies of blood. No amount of repellant seemed to work. John had brought a bug suit, and we had ridiculed him for looking like a beekeeper, but I coveted it dearly after a few hours on the trail. After three days of blood donations, we surrendered and made contact with our boat pickup to come out of the wilderness a few days early to go to Denali and try Halibut fishing out of Homer. Grewingk Glacier was our last spectacular spot before heading out.

The Sixpack in Alaska

We enjoyed seeing Denali National Park and saw many grizzly bears in the wild there. Three of us went on a fishing charter for Halibut, while the other three did a sea kayaking excursion to complete our last frontier experience.

Thanks to the great Alaska wilderness and my Sixpack council of advisors, I survived the ambush and was able to view the event from a larger perspective. I had much more processing to do and the final divorce proceedings yet to go through but being out in the elements in God's magnificent creation had given me a week of peace and reflection. I will be forever grateful for their support through my lowest valley.

When a Grizzly stands up to smell you, you're too close!

Life slams into each of us at some point. It is not possible to avoid challenges that threaten to derail you, can leave you bitter, and cast a shadow over your manhood. It might be the loss of a job, the failure of a marriage, a shocking diagnosis, a financial or family crisis. If you get nothing else from this book, remember this: our tendency as men is to retreat to the cave to be alone when we are hurting, but in order to heal properly, we must resist that urge to isolate and seek out fellowship. Develop friendships for the long haul. In good times these bring you great joy and fulfillment, and in times of trouble, these are the most valuable asset imaginable. Talking it out with someone you trust is cathartic. It helps you process so you can find your way forward and not get stuck in the pain. Having others to walk with you keeps you strong. Resilient. They've got your back and you've got theirs. Brotherhood at its best.

COURSE CORRECTION

Dealing well with heat, thirst, and sun protection in the desert makes you feel somewhat like a survival expert. However, just when you are confident you've got it mastered, you get thrown into an entirely new desert wilderness where you face bitter cold, loss of landmarks, and frostbite. This is exactly where I found myself at the end of 1999 on the eve of the new Millennium. I thought I was coping well with my "woman to love" purpose but found myself thrust into harsh new territory as a divorce statistic. I was well off the map—no landmarks, no guidance, no bearings. I was in pain and reverted to deep, old resentments against all women.

Hurting and angry, I sought solace in music. I love music and appreciate lyrics to songs. I believe the best album Bruce Springsteen ever put out was "Tunnel of Love" back in 1987. The musicality and storytelling of every song are superb. All are about love, but most are about love lost—something that Springsteen must have had a recent experience with. Summing up my predicament was the song "Spare Parts." The chorus goes like this:

Spare parts

And broken hearts

Keep the world turnin' around

These lyrics describe exactly how every family member feels after a marriage ends in divorce. You are a spare part. Sitting on a shelf. Hoping to be part of some greater whole again. From the same album, "Walk Like a Man" and "Brilliant Disguise" also resonated with me. I wasn't feeling too jazzed about the year 2000 and starting a new century.

Just to add an exclamation point, in February of 2000, my divorce was finalized with a trial. I had planned a trip to Cairo, Egypt, in May to visit a close friend and old fraternity brother on an ex-pat assignment with his family there. We were going to visit the ancient pyramids and do a river trip down the Nile, spotting hippos and crocodiles. It was just the kind of escape and additional perspective seeking that I needed. Once the divorce was finalized, I didn't expect money to be a problem to take the trip, but that was not how the assets were divided. I kept my retirement whole but lost all cash liquidity, so I had to cancel my trip to Egypt. BUMMER!

Since I was no longer living with my children and needed to increase my income to recover financially from the divorce, I decided to accept the promotion to North America Sales Manager on August 1, 2000. This job significantly increased my business travel. My good friend Damian Luna had done very well at the company and was our Business Unit's Global General Manager and my boss. Like Damian, many of my college fraternity brothers became lifelong relationships and provided me with tremendous support along the way. Life truly is a team sport!

I moved into the corporate apartment in Sugar Land, Texas, and immersed myself in work. My work to do purpose became central to my life at this point. The company had gone through a huge restructuring after the acquisition by Suez. Multiple business units were being combined or collapsed into one another, and our entire compensation system was being overhauled under a project titled COMP 2000, which I was asked to lead. I was going all over the country as well as the Caribbean Islands constructing new districts and pay systems. I had more or less decided that I would never remarry. I got deeply involved in politics and considered running for public office in later life. I planned to help out my children generationally through public service. This was really a foolish notion more than a plan. Who was I kidding? I was terribly lonely and never even in town except for every chance to have my kids. I had no time to look for a place to live, and I was approaching the limit on the time allowed for in the corporate apartment. I was living large on the expense account, traveling and having cocktails with all of my coworkers. On the outside, it might have looked like I was coping well, but I was at exactly the same spot in the cold new wilderness where the divorce had dumped me.

On one of my flights to the East Coast, a book review in the *USA Today* paper caught my eye. It was a book written by a husband-and-wife team of sociology professors at the University of Michigan, Amy and Leon Kass. The title of the book was *Wing to Wing, Oar to Oar:*

Readings on Courting and Marrying. I was engrossed by the title and drawn to the book even more as I read the review. Like the epiphany I had with the runaway at Philmont, I was having another moment of divine wisdom imparted to me. Here on this airplane, as I was crisscrossing the country evading my pain, God had found me and put that article in my hand to point me in a new direction, a direction which I felt certain was His will to obey. I purchased the book as soon as I hit the ground in New York.

The book was part of a series titled, "The Ethics of Everyday Life." The Preface states:

> This series has been produced by a group of friends, united by a concern for the basic moral aspects of our common life and by a desire to revive public interest in and attention to these matters, now sadly neglected ... We have been reading and writing, conversing and arguing, always looking for ways to deepen our own understanding of the meaning of human life as ordinarily lived, looking also for ways to enable others to join in the search. These anthologies of selected readings on various aspects of everyday life—courting and marrying, teaching and learning, working, leading, and dying—seem to us very well suited to the task.

The structure in the table of contents was set up as follows:

- Where Are We Now?

- Why Marry? Defense of Matrimony

- What About Sex? Man, Woman, and Sexuality

- Is This Love? Eros and Its Aims

- How Can I Find and Win the Right One? Courtship

- Why a Wedding? The Promises of Marriage

- What Can Married Life Be Like? The Blessings of Married Life

Here was the proverbial instruction manual on the subject I needed to learn about most! In each section, there were multiple offerings on the topic from the finest authors in history. What an incredible discovery! This book offered a new perspective on marriage with passionately worded arguments covering a tremendous span of time since the institution was created. I devoured the book and spent a great deal of time in self-examination as I read each section.

In 1982 when all the divorces were wrecking my family, I had developed a very warped perception of marriage. I needed to look at my journey and accept responsibility for the errors I had made, or I was destined to repeat them. It was time to get out the map, retrace my steps back to the point where I had taken the wrong trail, and rethink the whole purpose around finding a woman to love. This was going to be a huge course correction and would require heavy lifting.

Here is an excerpt from the Danish philosopher and theologian, Soren Kierkegaard written in 1845 entitled *Some Reflections on Marriage in Answer to Objections*:

> *My dear reader, if you do not have the time and opportunity to take a dozen years of your life to travel around the world to see everything a world traveler is acquainted with, if you do not have the capability and qualifications from years of practice in a foreign language to penetrate the differences in national characteristics as these become apparent to the research scholar, if you are not bent on discovering a new astronomical system that will displace both the Copernican*

*and the Ptolemaic—then marry; and if you have time for the first, the capability for the second, the idea for the last, then marry **also**. Even if you did not manage to see the whole globe or to speak in many tongues or to know all about the heavens, you will not regret it, for marriage is and remains the most important voyage of discovery a human being undertakes; compared with a married man's knowledge of life, any other knowledge of it is superficial, for he and he alone has properly immersed himself in life.*

WOW! Have you ever heard anyone today speak so highly of the institution of marriage!? This was unapologetic and passionate support for marriage. As I read other passages and eventually the entire book, I slowly turned in a totally new direction in my heart. I understood that it was indeed God's purpose for me to find a woman to love, and it was also His will to obey. My mistake in my initial marriage was my passivity about the process. I had not truly been searching with intentionality for the right person to marry in my twenties. I had not thought about a lifelong partnership and all that it means. I really didn't have a clear criterion of exactly what I was looking for, and when you don't have that, you cannot discern the difference between good and best. I prayed about this new path and asked God to show me how to do it right. I was wired for marriage by my Maker. It offers the fullest life possible at every level because our lives were meant to be shared with someone else. I decided that I now did, indeed, want to be married. In fact, I needed to be married to be happy. I had a clear vision of what I wanted. I had a specific criterion, and I would now go about my search intentionally looking for the best mate possible in every aspect of life.

COURSE CORRECTION

In September, I turned forty years old and began visiting churches around Houston with divorce recovery and singles programs. Most of the people I met in these groups were so wounded that they still needed years of therapy, and that is not where I felt I was in my situation. I didn't know many single people and certainly wasn't interested in the bar scene. I next began researching the new field of internet dating. One required an extensive series of surveys to define areas of compatibility. Then they matched you up with prospects in their membership where you had a high level of matching compatibility areas. This process appealed to the engineer in me, but it was expensive, and I was quite surprised at the high number of requests I was receiving and got into a pattern of many first dates but not much follow up to go on a second one. Perhaps the next one was better? I dropped that membership and got help again from above.

Every day I drove to my office in our Division Headquarters in Sugar Land, I passed a big billboard right before I turned into our driveway for the office. On that billboard it said, "Meet Quality Singles at ChristianSingleWeb.com." Come on now, a book review in a newspaper and now a billboard right in front of my office? These were, literally, bolts of lightning sent from on high! I can be a slow learner, but I am not totally unobservant. I made an appointment to go check it out. Another great irony was that the building where the Christian Single Web office was located was the same building where my first job was with Turner Collie & Braden Consulting Engineers! I had course-corrected on my journey back to the same physical address where my professional career began back in 1982! I knew that being a believing Christian was number one on my must-have list for a prospective spouse and thought that this was the perfect pond to go fish in for the right species. I joined on the spot, filled out my profile, and was filmed for my online video profile.

I promised myself that I would make Mr. Heath, my old Scoutmaster who made me carry the #5 can around camp, proud of how courteous I planned to be in truly courting any prospect for a successful marriage. I would refrain from sexual temptation and attempt to become a friend before a lover. I was also pleased to learn that this organization had events where members could get together for social events as a group without it being a date. I felt this would also help me build some new male friendships with other single men. I didn't have any at the time.

It wasn't long before I received my first invitation from an extremely attractive woman who had seen my profile and offered to console me on a recent A&M football game loss. Her name was Kimberly McClard. She was divorced and raising two boys on her own, Geoffrey and Shaun. We agreed to meet at a local Mexican restaurant called Tortugas for an early dinner on October 13, 2000. I was there early and stood behind the hostess stand at the bar. When she walked in, I was immediately smitten by her radiant smile and cute little Kirk Douglas dimple in her chin. I honestly could not believe that she was the one who had sent the invitation to me. She seemed out of my league—sweet, beautiful, and kind. I could go on at length about our courtship, but that could be a book all by itself. All I knew was that I was certain she was God's provision for me when I chose to obey His will.

Fortunately, we shared a common chemistry for one another. My work travel actually helped us get to know each other better through email correspondence, and I was extremely courteous. I wrote her poems and waited until our third or fourth date before I even attempted a kiss. Then I wrote her the following poem about it.

OUR FIRST KISS

A lunch at mid-day, hardly a tryst,
Was the plot that I hatched for our first kiss.
I'd imagined its sweetness, gentle and soft,
As I'd lay in my bed and slowly drift off.

What was it about her that affected me so?
We had met over dinner just a short week ago.
I pondered her spell and how it was cast,
Was it those brown eyes, or the lilt in her laugh?

No matter the method, in my mind I was snared.
*I simply **must** kiss her wherever I dared!*
Would it be at her office as I walked her in,
With coworkers teasing and hiding their grins?

It turned out quite naturally, before she stepped from the car
When my longing was answered, like a wish on a star.
With a sigh it was over, one is never enough,
But the pleasure still lingers until next our lips touch.

I never went on another date with anyone else from ChristianSingleWeb.com, but I felt my investment had paid off handsomely. We grew closer and closer and fell in love. We both were very careful about introducing one another to our children because we knew that was going to be a big moment for everyone. The following May, on her fortieth birthday, I proposed to her at Morton's Restaurant with another poem. We were engaged for a full year and then got married on June 1, 2002.

The Sixpack at our wedding with camping hats

Admitting that you are lost is a difficult decision to make for a prideful man. That is why there are so many jokes about men refusing to stop and ask for directions. My first marriage was flawed from the beginning from many of my own mistakes. I became sexually intimate much too early in the relationship, which made the compatibility red flags easier to ignore. I knew that we had big differences in religion and culture, being from very different backgrounds. I was passive about discussing those and about almost every aspect of planning our wedding. I was not intentional about pursuing marriage and didn't have a vision of what I wanted it to look like. It was similar to looking out a long way into the night sky with a telescope. When amplified across a great distance, a single tiny degree can put you on a completely different planet, one that you did not intend to visit. I acknowledged my navigational error, admitted that I was lost, and went back to my compass, God's will, to fix a new destination. I had to hike a long way back and give up a lot of elevation to end up back at that office on Woodway Drive in Houston, Texas. I was then intentional about what I wanted and took the steps needed to search for it. Once I

Our engagment photo

found her, I was courteous and took my time to be certain I landed the catch of a lifetime!

Finding a woman to love is written into our DNA code. God is a God of family. He created male and female in the beginning, with a clear purpose in mind. Not just for procreation, but also for companionship. Partnership. A lot of us get it wrong for whatever reason. Maybe it wasn't modeled well for us growing up. Maybe we approached it too casually and dived in too quickly, driven mostly by our hormones. Maybe we got self-absorbed along the way and didn't nurture it as much as we needed to. It is easy for marriage to go wrong—but it is really worth getting it right. It is worth discussing with our sons and nephews and younger co workers. At a time when masculinity is considered toxic and chivalry is considered chauvinistic, it is *still* worth whatever effort is required to be a man worthy of being loved by a good woman. Providing for her. Protecting her. Championing her and making sure she knows every day that she is loved and cherished.

Wherever you are on the relationship spectrum right now, I encourage you to consider the blessings of finding a woman to love and keeping that love healthy and vibrant for a lifetime.

C H A P T E R   F I F T E E N

THE BOOMERANG
OF KINDNESS

It will probably come as no surprise to my reader that my favorite television show is related to survival and self-reliance in the outdoors. The show is called "ALONE" and is aired on the History Channel. The basic concept is ten survival experts are dropped off in separate extremely remote locations and must survive with only the backpack full of items they are allowed to bring. They must build a shelter and hunt, fish, or forage for all of their food. They are given some training on how to film themselves and provided video equipment and a cache of batteries. They are also given GPS beacons that allow them to call for help in an emergency or when they want to "tap out" or be picked up. They are totally alone for the entire series and are unaware of others tapping out until they become the sole survivor to win the prize money.

This show fascinates me on multiple levels. First, it is just interesting to see what kind of people are willing to put themselves through such a severe challenge. Most are already experts in survival skills but the psychological aspect of denying yourself any other human contact for up to one hundred days is something difficult to prepare yourself for mentally. Watching the participants build shelters and begin to determine what they will eat is equally intriguing. The show has completed seven full seasons, so newer participants have watched previous episodes and observed different approaches. There is a balance one must strike between calorie expenditure versus calorie intake. Building a superior shelter will demand you to expend a lot more energy than fabricating something simpler. Likewise, fishing with a gill net is a much lower energy demand than stalking and hunting game. Finally, the change in the behavior of the participants throughout the season is gripping as they become silly and more conversant with the camera because of their longing for social interaction. Some of the very best participants at attaining adequate food sources succumb to loneliness and tap out for psychological or homesick reasons. In the final episode, a spouse or other close family member or friend greets the winner by surprise to let them know that they are the final one left in the wilderness and have won the prize for that season.

I mention this show because when you backpack a lot, you encounter people like this somewhat frequently. They are on some quest to examine themselves or prove something to themselves or others, and they have chosen to do it alone. Many times, these people have seriously underestimated the impact that loneliness might have on them. They usually want to talk when you encounter them. Sometimes when you are hiking with a group and do not have the same longings, you can be quick to dismiss these people. After all, most of us have retreated to the woods to get away from others. However, information is important in the backcountry, and there are no newspapers. You might need information like water source locations or to check in on a trailhead bear warning where you intend to camp. We always ask about fishing details like bait or flies and certainly about distances and difficulty of trail conditions. Some folks are chatty, and others will barely grunt a hello as they march on by. But kindness and sensitivity to others' needs somehow increase when you are placed in a situation of scarcity. You could very easily be that person in need.

On our Alaska excursion, we cut our backpack trip short due to the severe bug infestation. Joe, Adolph, and I were fishing along a river full of pink Salmon near Homer the first day we had come off the trail. While we were trying our luck, we encountered a young Japanese man angling in the same area. His English wasn't very good, but he was extremely eager to talk to other fishermen. He had been by himself for weeks already, and we could see that he needed company badly. With gestures and a good deal of repetition, we communicated that we planned to hire a guide the next day to go out fishing for Halibut. He became very excited, so we asked him if he would like to join us. He practically hugged us and became very animated. It didn't seem like much to us, but he kept bowing and thanking us profusely. We told him where to meet us at the marina and how much it would cost and told him to meet us there in the morning at the appointed time.

He was there at the marina waiting for us like a little kid going on his first trip with grandpa. We could plainly see that this experience was something very special for him, so we slapped him on the back and treated him like one of our own. We caught a lot of big Halibut and high fived each other on a beautiful day out on the water. His big grin was infectious and constant throughout the day, and we took a picture of our catch with him and two other men who came on our boat to fill it. I don't remember his name, but I do know that he appreciated that special day being with other people who loved to do something that he loved to do but might not have been able to communicate well enough to arrange the charter or get others to go with him so he could afford it. Being kind to that young man was something very simple and easy for us to do, but it clearly made a tremendous impact on him and his ability to live out a dream for a day. Adolph, Joe, and I felt warm inside all evening as we dined on fresh Halibut with the other three from our crew for dinner.

Our proud Japanese fishing companion (far right)

We encountered another lone hiker more recently on our trip to Glacier National Park. In the National Parks, you must secure a permit to camp at established campgrounds to minimize impact on the park. This limits your privacy but increases your interaction with other hikers. We had just finished setting up camp and were finalizing our decision to head out a day early due to snow in the forecast for the last day. A young woman by herself came into camp looking quite dejected and tired. We welcomed her and offered her some of our better snacks, which she gladly accepted. She sat down on a log by our fire, and we began exchanging pleasantries about where we were from, where we were going, and what brought us to Glacier NP.

The other guys were teasing me about my birthday the next day and how we were all getting a bit long in the tooth. I think she said something about her dad's birthday being in September as well. That led to a story about a rift in her relationship with her father. She had finished college and taken a job to teach English as a second language in Korea. She told us that she had met another young American teacher at the school doing the same thing, a young man. They had gotten serious, but when the assignment was over, he broke off the relationship. She was heartbroken and returned to the U.S. but didn't want to go home to face her father yet, so this introspective quest to Glacier was intended to give her time to sort herself out. She had been out a few days and taken a tumble and was slightly bruised and scraped. She told us that she had taken off her backpack to do a side hike somewhere and that the chipmunks had gotten into all of her food, and she was unsure about eating anything left. She unwrapped a block of cheese with lots of tiny teeth marks on it. The dad in all of us immediately rushed to comfort this poor creature. We shared our dinner and then gave her all of our food except for breakfast the next day, explaining that we were heading out early and wanted to drop the weight for the hike out. Could she please help us out with that? She looked so relieved. She was clearly hungry and had planned a minimal amount of food to begin with but was too proud to ask for anything.

I started talking to her about being a father to my own young adult children. I admitted to her that maybe I had made some mistakes or been too hard on them in certain situations. Our whole crew assured her that we deeply loved our children and always felt badly when there was a disagreement. We explained that we were certain her father was longing to see her after being in Korea for two years, and whatever their disagreement had been, he would be craving restoration and forgiveness from both sides. I remember her face as we talked. She was staring into the flickering flames of the fire with wide and just slightly moist eyes. As we completed our defense of father screw-ups, she smiled broadly for the first time, a beautiful smile. We said good night as the wind was picking up from the front, moving in to bring the snow.

We got up early the next morning, ready to beat the storm out to the trailhead. That morning my job was to go down to the lake's edge to collect and sterilize our water for the day. As I walked down, I saw an unusual pattern in the sea of rocks along the shore. I wasn't sure what I was seeing at first but then recognized it as a kind of mosaic. The picture below is what I saw.

A heartwarming Happy Birthday

The young woman had already left camp when we looked around for her. She must have hunted those rocks out with a flashlight the night before, or I just missed her after she rose at the crack of dawn to leave me that birthday wish down by the water. This small gesture, which cost nothing, moved me in a big way. It was unexpected and essentially from a stranger, but it had required careful thought, time, and creativity. Our fatherly kindness and recognition of her need were repaid, and we were both richly rewarded.

Although we needled each other mercilessly within the Sixpack on our adventures, when a legitimate need arose, we were also kind to one another. On one of our trips into the Wind River range, I was fishing along a steep bluff and hooked a good-sized Cutthroat. I climbed down closer to the water on a six-inch ledge to grab him by the lip since we didn't carry nets. With my rod in my right hand bent like an upside-down J, I reached with my left hand to secure the fish. Just as I did, I heard a loud "TWANG" as the grasshopper lure released from his mouth, and the tension from the rod tip yanked the hook deep into my left ring finger just below the joint. Even the smallest injuries in the backcountry become more serious due to infection risk, and I knew this was going to be a problem. Besides that, it hurt like hell, and I really wanted to get that hook out of my finger. I pulled out my mini-Leatherman tool and tried to tug it out myself. OW! The barb on the hook was not going to allow that to happen. The hook was not even visible,

I got hooked, but I was able to keep the catch

and it looked like I had a grasshopper being birthed out of my finger with the blood.

Adolph was nearby, and I asked him to take a look at the situation. After dropping down the magnifiers on his glasses he used to tie his fishing knots, he assessed the predicament and gave a long "Hmmmm…."

"Dave, it looks like we'll have to push the hook all the way through your finger to be able to clip the barb off with the Leatherman tool once we get it out on the other side."

Not exactly the diagnosis I had hoped for, to be sure! But I really had no other choice. Fingers have lots of nerve endings, and this was a somewhat excruciating field surgery experience, but Adolph was being as kind and caring as he could be in these circumstances. I was trying to push the whole grasshopper through my finger, it seemed, and he kept saying, "Push a little more; I can't see the barb yet."

"Wait a minute! I can see it now!"

I heard a loud "SNIP" and thought he had done it.

"Nope, didn't get the barb yet. Just got the tip."

"Oh, my God!" I exclaimed.

"Push one more time and hold it flush as you can."

I heard another "SNIP," and then he showed me the tiny piece of metal proudly.

I was able to back the hook out of the entry wound without tearing any muscle or damaging any nerves, thankfully. He then tenderly bandaged me up and claimed that we were now even.

"What do you mean, now even?" I asked.

He said, "You saved my life on the first trip in the Weminuche Wilderness, and now I have saved yours."

We still joke about both to this day.

We all need a little kindness at one time or another. It seems a little easier to give it when you recognize that you may not be very far from needing it yourself. That is the great equalizer of the wilderness. We are all just simple hikers on our journey into the mountains where our weaknesses and vulnerabilities are certain to be exposed. The more aware you are of others' needs and respond by helping, this kindness will be returned to you more often than not. Kindness has a boomerang effect. We all need to build up our capital in our kindness accounts!

WE ALL NEED A LITTLE KINDNESS
AT ONE TIME OR ANOTHER.

CHAPTER SIXTEEN

PASSING THE TORCH

When Kim and I got married in 2002, our four children were sixteen, fourteen, twelve, and ten years old. My new stepsons, Geoffrey and Shaun, were the oldest, followed by Nicole and Dayton as the youngest. We were a new "blended family." Geoffrey and Shaun lived in Katy with Kim and me, while Nicole and Dayton followed the state law standard in divorce decrees for visitation: every other weekend and Wednesday evenings. An entire book could be written about our stepfamily experience, but that is not the purpose of this chapter or book. I will point you toward another great resource we found by Ron Deal, who did write a book on the topic called *The Smart Stepfamily.*

Kim and I bought our new house in Katy, and when we had them all together, we were dragging all four kids around to visit churches. They detested the experience of being the new kids at every church we visited. Kim had been a member of a Baptist church, and I had been a member of a Methodist church previously. We wanted to find an "ours" church, so we visited quite a few. In the end, the Baptist church that Kim had been affiliated with was starting up a new Stepfamily Bible Study Class beginning with a homegroup and using Ron Deal's book as a study guide. We joined Second Baptist as our church, and all six of us were baptized again, together, to recommit ourselves to Christ. I became one of the teachers of the new stepfamily Bible study class, now dubbed "The Zoo."

Geoffrey and Shaun had been living with their mom for almost seven years since her divorce and were unaccustomed to any adult male in the house. Nicole and Dayton didn't live with us, so our ability to impact them in a meaningful way was limited. They lived in the Woodlands, and all of their friends and school activities were up there. I felt extremely challenged to try to parent all four of our children in the way that I felt was best and also in a way that they would receive it. I knew I had to be very intentional and strategic in my approach to prepare them rapidly for independent adult life. Kim and I both hoped for a good grounding in faith as the most important thing we could model and teach.

A series of deaths in the family among the fathers soon after we got married left us all reeling. Kim's stepfather Richard was diagnosed with kidney cancer and passed away in 2004. Geoffrey and Shaun's biological father passed away from liver failure in 2005. And my father passed away in 2006 after battling lung cancer. As seemingly the last man standing, I felt the weight of being the only role model my three boys had to look to as an example. Shaun and Geoffrey were seriously struggling with the loss of their father so early in their young lives and were not ready to accept me as any kind of replacement. They were also close to Richard, and losing them both so close together, on top of adjusting to a new authority figure in their home, demanded more coping skills than they had. They both sought unhealthy ways to cope.

I had read the book *Raising a Modern Day Knight* by Robert Lewis and had also heard of a new outdoor father and son adventure program that he had developed called "Christ in the Tetons." It was not inexpensive, but it sounded fantastic. Their website today describes it thusly:

> *Our Father and Son Adventures are fantastic weeklong experiences full of fun, laughter, and excitement set in spectacular Jackson Hole, Wyoming. Activities include climbing, rafting, hiking, exploring, and much more, including great food and excellent accommodations. Join us for an experience that focuses on a man's wild and adventurous heart and the awesome power of the father and son relationship. Together, you will create priceless memories, strengthen your relationship, and discover God's great adventure for your lives.* (christinthetetons.com)

I decided that this trip could provide the kind of highly valued ceremony like I had experienced in scouting days when the Medicine Man inducted scouts into the Brotherhood of Cheerful Service and bring each son and me closer together through a one-on-one experience together. I decided that I would take each boy upon their high school completion and make a big deal of the trip. Geoffrey had graduated in 2004, but I hadn't discovered the program at that time, so near the beginning of the year in 2006, I posed it to him this way: "Geoffrey, how would you like to go to Jackson Hole Wyoming and go whitewater rafting on the Snake River, attend the Exum Climbing School in Grand Tetons National Park, and visit Yellowstone National Park?"

Rock climbing at the Exum Climbing School

He said, "Wow! Sounds fantastic!"

I replied, "There are only two catches: first, you have to go with me; and second, it is called Christ in the Tetons."

He didn't flinch. He had never been taken on any big outdoor adventure and was excited about the trip from that first moment. We went in late July 2006. I received news of my father passing away while we were still in Jackson Hole on August 6, which made it an even more emotionally charged event. That trip changed the dynamic of our relationship tremendously and still ranks as one of the very best decisions I have ever made.

Shaun was struggling even more with the loss of his father and was very put off by church in any capacity. Losing his father and grandfather back-to-back had made him very angry with God—if he even still believed in Him. He was having substance abuse problems during his senior year of high school and ended up failing a drug test at school that Fall. It was a rocky time, and we insisted that he join a treatment program called Adolescents in Recovery or AIR. He faked it for a while, then found a friend to live with before he graduated so he could bail on the program. He was out of contact with us from May through December of 2007 when he wanted to come home. We agreed to let him come home only if he re-entered the AIR program. He did agree and then truly worked on processing all of the pain he had experienced in his young life. Kim and I became deeply involved with the program, and we all attended three meetings a week in addition to individual counseling for the next two years. Shaun completed the program, and in a very touching ceremony called his "Awakening," he publicly told his whole story to a room full of people.

I was still very determined to take Shaun to Christ in the Tetons, but he was not interested whatsoever. The AIR program leader worked on me regarding this goal. She said it was my goal and not his. We should be pleased with his recovery and allow him to choose his own special way to celebrate it with me one on one. Shaun and I both love music, especially live music. Kim had taken both of us to the Austin City Limits Music Festival one year for his birthday present and had a great time. Instead of Christ in the Tetons, he wanted to go to the Coachella Music Festival near Palm Springs, California. It was nothing like what I had planned to have, a more structured plan with Christ's teaching at its center as our way to connect. But I agreed because I wanted a closer relationship with Shaun, and I thought a Coachella trip to California could be the breakthrough we needed.

It was a fantastic time for both of us. We flew into Los Angeles, rented a convertible Mustang, and went directly to an In and Out Burger for his first California experience. We went down to the Santa Monica Pier and muscle beach. Shaun wanted to get a tattoo at LA Ink, some place he had heard about from a television show. He proposed that we both get a tattoo of a camel on our butts to commemorate our trip together. "A Camel?" I asked.

"Yes, because a camel begins and ends every day on his knees and tries to go all day without taking a drink!"

I actually considered the idea but could not go through with it. I did like the symbolism, though.

I sprang for VIP tickets to the festival, so we had an exceptional experience listening to bands and checking out all the large-scale artwork around the grounds. We talked a lot and achieved the goal of becoming closer over the trip.

All smiles at the Coachella Music Festival

I took Dayton to Christ in Tetons in 2009, and we also became much closer through the special experience. At the end of each Tetons trip, we had a special knighting ceremony with a big sword and shield. There was also a ceremony where the participants were given a pewter benchmark to commemorate the experience. A USGS benchmark can be found on all of the mountain peaks around the U.S., so it is a fitting symbol for achieving a high point in your life. I've included a photo of my two benchmarks from the two Christ in the Tetons experience and a Serenity Prayer engraved on a similar size piece of pewter to represent the journey Shaun and I shared.

My special one-on-one trophies with my sons

I took Nicole on a father-daughter cruise for our special one on one trip after her high school graduation in 2008. Regardless of how many children you have, every father should take the time to make each child feel special with some individual one on one time. The dividends will last a lifetime!

Behind a strong faith foundation, my second big priority in attempting to pass the torch to our family's next generation was to educate them more on love and lasting relationships. Kim and I had failed in our prior marriages, and our children had suffered the consequences of those failures as innocent bystanders. All four of them were naturally reluctant even to discuss the topic of marriage. I knew my own warped perception of marriage from the divorces in my family had put me off for years on the prospect. However, people are not created to go through life alone. How could I teach them about my mistakes so that they could avoid the same thing? If there is a single wish I could have granted for my children, it would be never to have to experience divorce again as a spouse. I wanted to warn them about the temptations and trials that might test them in a marriage.

I WANTED TO TEACH MY CHILDREN ABOUT MY MISTAKES SO THAT THEY COULD AVOID REPEATING THE SAME THINGS.

I discovered another great book only recently, but I wish I had found it much earlier. The title of the book is *The Seven Deadly Sins Today* by Henry Fairlie. The book was written in 1979 before the internet or iPhones were invented but spookily prevenient regarding such tools today. If you have never heard of the seven deadly sins, they were named such by Pope Gregory the Great in the Middle Ages, and they are given in a certain order. They are:

1. Pride

2. Envy

3. Anger

4. Sloth

5. Avarice (or Greed)

6. Gluttony

7. Lust

Here is a brief excerpt from the first chapter, "The Fact of Sin":

We are dealing with an elaborate intellectual construction that is intended to illustrate profound moral truths. All the Seven Deadly Sins are demonstrations of love that has gone wrong. They spring from the impulse, which is natural in man, to love what pleases him, but the love is misplaced or weakened or distorted ... Pride and Envy and Anger are sins of <u>perverted love</u>. The love is directed to a worthy object—in each case to oneself—but it is directed in a false manner. The fault in them is that one imagines that one may gain some good for oneself by causing harm to others. Sloth is placed next as a sin of <u>defective love</u>. The love may be directed to a deserving object, but it is not given in proper measure. Avarice and Gluttony and Lust are sins of <u>excessive love</u>. The love again may be directed to what in themselves are deserving objects, but it is so excessive that it interrupts and must, in the end, destroy one's capacity to love other objects that are also and perhaps even more deserving.

I found this wisdom profound. Truthfully, I believe that this is the best book I have ever read of any kind. It is so penetrating and honest in its discussion of our human nature and the elaborate rationalizations of our sinful behavior. It is also critical of psychiatry and of the excuses it finds for us. With three of our four children now thirty or older, I am having more meaningful conversations on an adult-to-adult level where I can share wisdom and pass that torch which lights the way to minimizing the pain they might have to experience in life through learning the hard way.

Another resource from Robert Lewis was the Men's Fraternity program called "The Quest for Authentic Manhood." This curriculum sets out to answer some questions that are universal to men.

- What makes a man a man? A real man?
- How does one become a real man?
- Is there a moment when it happens?
- What is it that holds men back from their true masculine destiny?
- How should authentic manhood express itself today?

I facilitated this program in our "Zoo" stepfamily class, with the product being written manhood plans for those who completed the full curriculum. This material was first developed by Robert in 1990 and has reached millions worldwide since. In 2015, Robert rebranded and relaunched the Christ in the Tetons program in combination with relaunching Men's Fraternity, calling both programs "Adventures for Life" with the sole mission of Better Men, Better Dads. The new father and son adventure was called "Journey to Manhood" and reduced to three days so that it was accessible to more people and could be done in any outdoor setting. The Quest for Authentic Manhood was rebranded Man to Man and has now combined with other men's ministries to be called "BetterMan." I have been an avid supporter of each of these programs as they have polished and distilled their content to the essence of what young men need today. In fact, it has been this program and the need I sense among today's young men that has put the burden on my heart to write this book. I list in the Appendix how to access these resources.

My intent has been to chart my own stumbling and bumbling path through the wilderness and share transparently where I experienced failure and success. I have had to acknowledge the moments when I was lost and outside of God's will, acting in my own will. I have had to course-correct on my woman to love purpose. And I have shared where I reoriented myself through God's divine guidance to be successful in my work to do. I hope that it can help you on your own journey, and I challenge you to pass the torch to keep lighting the way for our next generation of men.

Dayton's Christ in the Tetons Manhood Ceremony

CONCLUSION

In concluding this memoir, I'd like to take you back to all those weeks at summer camp as a youth and boy scout in West Texas when my masculinity was just beginning to take shape. It was a tradition at our summer camp to close the campfire program with a song called the Scout Vespers. Here are the lyrics:

Softly falls the light of day
As our campfire fades away
Silently each scout should ask,
"Have I done my daily task?"
"Have I kept my honor bright?"
"Can I, guiltless, sleep tonight?"
"Have I done? And have I dared?"
"Everything to be prepared?"

Each troop or patrol would be dismissed silently while those remaining hummed the melody until the last group filed off. I would take those words to heart each summer, asking myself those very questions as I rolled around on my cot, trying to fall asleep in the warm West Texas summer night.

Even today, I cannot overstate the positive impact that the Boy Scouts of America has had on my life. I personally revere the title Eagle Scout because of the extremely high ideals it asked of me early on in my life. The BSA left an indelible mark on me and provided the best possible foundation for what I believe is a healthy, positive masculinity. For those of you who may not have had the opportunity to be involved with the BSA program as a youth, I'd like to share the core tenets of the program with you from the BSA website:

SCOUT OATH

On my honor, I will do my best to do my duty to God and my country and to obey the Scout Law; to help other people at all times; to keep myself physically strong, mentally awake, and morally straight.

SCOUT LAW

The Scout Law has 12 points. Each is a goal for every Scout. A Scout tries to live up to the Law every day. It is not always easy to do, but a Scout always tries.

A SCOUT IS:

- **TRUSTWORTHY.** Tell the truth and keep promises. People can depend on you.

- **LOYAL.** Show that you care about your family, friends, Scout leaders, school, and country.

- **HELPFUL.** Volunteer to help others without expecting a reward.

- **FRIENDLY.** Be a friend to everyone, even people who are very different from you.

- **COURTEOUS.** Be polite to everyone and always use good manners.

- **KIND.** Treat others as you want to be treated. Never harm or kill any living thing without good reason.

- **OBEDIENT.** Follow the rules of your family, school, and pack. Obey the laws of your community and country.

- **CHEERFUL.** Look for the bright side of life. Cheerfully do tasks that come your way. Try to help others be happy.

- **THRIFTY.** Work to pay your own way. Try not to be wasteful. Use time, food, supplies, and natural resources wisely.

- **BRAVE.** Face difficult situations even when you feel afraid. Do what you think is right despite what others might be doing or saying.

- **CLEAN.** Keep your body and mind fit. Help keep your home and community clean.

- **REVERENT.** Be reverent toward God. Be faithful in your religious duties. Respect the beliefs of others.

All twelve principles of the Scout Law were touched on in the chapters of this book. In fact, it was the initial inspiration for the book to acknowledge their importance in my character development. Consider what you have read and see if you can identify which of these twelve points highlights a particular chapter. I purposely did not put them in the official order, so this source of inspiration would not be immediately obvious.

I salute and thank the Boy Scouts of America for their Oath, their Motto "Be Prepared," and these twelve points of the Scout Law. I was richly blessed with many great experiences and relationships and remain proud to call myself an Eagle Scout and Philmont Ranger. This fine organization has been under attack and taken to court repeatedly for decades now. Why anyone would want to tear down such a valuable organization involved in raising better young men simply escapes me. I remember what it was and have tried to preserve some of that by writing this memoir so others might have a record of what it was intended to be.

Scouting was the large early influence on my journey through the wilderness, and it opened the door to a special group of men who wanted to continue backpacking adventures as adults for as long as we are able. Throughout much of this book, I have related stories from my early years in scouting and adult years backpacking in the mountains. I have suggested that a campfire can become, and often is, a sacred place for genuine sharing and experiencing the most intimate fellowship possible. I would like to return now to the campfire as a metaphor, but this time in reference to an old Eskimo Proverb that goes like this:

Yesterday is wood

Tomorrow is ashes

Only today does the fire burn brightly

The simple wisdom in this is clear. We cannot change the past or control the future. In fact, we are in different physical states using this metaphor. Only today can we act, while the fire burns brightly, to live in the moment, to take the risks and enjoy the rewards of authentic manhood and true fellowship. It is a warm, luminous, and cheerful place where the fire burns brightly! If I have gained any trust from you at all through this trip through my wilderness experience, please believe me when I say that this journey can never be successful if undertaken alone. Life and manhood, in particular, is a team sport!

Finally, I believe our Maker has a common purpose for every man, to accompany and compliment his specific gifted purpose. It's time to share my own Report Card at this milestone in my life.

Here are the subjects along with my grade and any additional comment:

- **FIND A WORK TO DO:** This was my best subject. A-

- **FIND A WOMAN TO LOVE:** I failed and had to retake. F

  Remarkable Improvement Version 2.0. A+

- **FIND A WILL TO OBEY:** I had brilliant spurts but numerous pride setbacks. C+

  Showing Wisdom Accrual Now – Solid B

Writing this book was an intentional surrender to God's will. My journey is far from over as I step into new roles—new work to do—like being a grandfather and have just made a place in our home for my mother-in-law to live with us.

In keeping with the school metaphor, I will leave you, my reader, with the following homework assignment:

REFLECT

Listen to two songs for me and closely pay attention to the lyrics. Pull them up on a lyrics website and read them as you listen to focus on understanding and relating to the artist's feelings performing each song. The two songs are:

- **"Father of Mine"** by Everclear

- **"Drive (For Daddy Gene)"** by Alan Jackson

After listening to both songs, decide between the two about which song's kind of a man you want to be. Then take the following three steps:

- **ONE:** Determine where you are on your journey toward authentic manhood. Fix your current position on the wilderness map wherever it is and, be brutally honest about it.

- **TWO:** Decide that this journey is well worth taking to live your very best life and plan a route to your desired destination. There will inevitably be reroutes and backtracks, but a plan is required to begin moving in the right direction.

- **THREE:** Seek out and actively recruit other men to go on this journey with you. If possible, look for older, more experienced men who can act as a guide and share their wisdom with you about where the hazards lie. All the advice in the world is useless unless heeded.

And if you are truly brave, take this fourth step:

- **FOUR:** Go to my website thesavagepath.com and publicly post your choice to herald a formal beginning to your best possible life.

BEING A MALE IS A MATTER
OF BIRTH. BEING A MAN IS
A MATTER OF CHOICE.

—EDWIN LOUIS COLE

APPENDIX

If you need resources to help you along the way, I have listed some of the excellent materials I have found invaluable along my path. Anyone who has backpacked as much as I have understands the value of trekking poles and maintaining three points of contact when crossing treacherous terrain. These resources and tools are your trekking poles on this journey. And finally, be proud of yourself for making the effort to be a healthy, strong, and masculine man that our nation and world so badly needs to deal with its many problems today.

I invite you to continue visiting my website for updates, blogs, and new content as we increase our resources to support the quest for positive, healthy masculinity.

REFERENCE BOOKS:

- *Raising a Modern Day Knight* by Robert Lewis

- *Every Man's Battle: Every Man's Guide to Winning the War on Sexual Temptation One Victory at a Time* by Stephen Arterburn and Fred Stoker

- *Wing to Wing, Oar to Oar: Readings on Courting and Marrying* by Amy A. Kass and Leon R. Kass

- *Whispers in the Wilderness* by Erik Stensland

- *The Seven Deadly Sins Today* by Henry Fairlie

- *The Call: Finding and Fulfilling the Central Purpose of Your Life* by Os Guiness

- *The Men's Fraternity Bible* by Holman Bible Publishers

- *Work With Passion: How to Do What You Love for a Living* by Nancy Anderson

- *The Smart Stepfamily* by Ron Deal

GOOD SEED CHOKED OUT BY THORNS

I am back in western Texas feeling closer to my roots
Where shafts of sunlight pierce the clouds,
like a searchlight on the butte
At dusk, it's still and quiet, only insects chirping low
As I strain to hear the still, small voice; His will for me to know

In the din of the city with its lusts, deceits, and fears
I'm lost and feel quite distant from the One I should be near
I don't want to be the seed choked out by all the thorns
Succumbing to the Evil One, whose schemes against I'm warned

The troubles of this world, like fiery darts against me fly
The shield of faith, my only hope, in thwarting all his lies
I long to go on offense, taking back the ground I've lost
But a single soldier army, like a cork at sea is tossed

Lord, please help me remember, it's Your grace and not my will
That unleashes heavenly power and provides us with the skill
To stand against the devil and to bear the fruit You planned
To cling to your true message and bring healing to our land

—DLS 11/11/14

STAND TRUE TO YOUR
CALLING TO BE A MAN.
REAL WOMEN WILL
ALWAYS BE RELIEVED AND
GRATEFUL WHEN MEN ARE
WILLING TO BE MEN.

—ELISABETH ELLIOTT

STUDY GUIDE

CHAPTER ONE
COURAGE/BRAVERY

SCRIPTURE—JOSHUA 1:9

"I command you—be strong and courageous! Do not be afraid or discouraged. For the Lord your God is with you wherever you go."

DISCUSSION QUESTIONS

1. When was a time when you had to be courageous?

2. Who taught you how to be brave?

3. Was there a time you were not brave, and you now regret this?

CHAPTER TWO
THRIFTY/RESOURCEFUL

SCRIPTURE—PROVERBS 13:4

*"Lazy people want much but get little, but those
who work hard will prosper and be satisfied."*

DISCUSSION QUESTIONS

1. When did you first show an aptitude toward a vocation?

2. Do you have trouble managing money or expenses now? Why do you think this is? If yes, how could you get back on track?

3. Share from a time when you were resourceful to solve a problem.

C H A P T E R   T H R E E
CEREMONY / REVERENT

SCRIPTURE—MATTHEW 3:16-17

"After his baptism, Jesus came up out of the water, the heavens were opened, and he saw the Spirit of God descending like a dove and settling on him. And a voice from heaven said, 'This is my beloved Son, and I am fully pleased with him.'"

DISCUSSION QUESTIONS

1. Do you have a significant ceremony memory? (Baptism, marriage, military honor. etc.)

2. What made that ceremony feel memorable?

3. Can you describe a time when you believe you became a man?

CHAPTER FOUR
OBEDIENT

SCRIPTURE—1 SAMUEL 15:22

"But Samuel replied, 'What is more pleasing to the Lord: your burnt offerings and sacrifices or your obedience to his voice? Obedience is far better than sacrifice. Listening to him is much better than offering the fat of rams.'"

DISCUSSION QUESTIONS

1. Have you, or do you still, struggle with authority? What do you believe might be the root cause of this issue in yourself or others?

2. Can you share an example of when your obedience was rewarded?

3. What do you think makes men want to rebel against authority?

C H A P T E R F I V E
FRIENDLY

SCRIPTURE—PROVERBS 17:17

*"A friend is always loyal, and a brother
is born to help in time of need."*

DISCUSSION QUESTIONS

1. How many friends have you had for more than ten years?

2. Is it easy or difficult for you to make new friends? Why?

3. What does it take to keep friends for a long time?

C H A P T E R   S I X
LOYALTY

SCRIPTURE—1 CHRONICLES 12:33

"From the tribe of Zebulun, there were 50,000 skilled
warriors. They were fully armed and prepared
for battle and completely loyal to David."

DISCUSSION QUESTIONS

1. Provide an example of when you were loyal to a friend.

2. What does it feel like when someone is disloyal to you?

3. What are some examples of the rewards of loyalty?

CHAPTER SEVEN
PERSEVERANCE / ENDURANCE

SCRIPTURE—JAMES 1:2-4

"Dear brothers and sisters, whenever trouble comes your way, let it be an opportunity for joy. For when your faith is tested, your endurance has a chance to grow. So let it grow, for when your endurance is fully developed, you will be strong in character and ready for anything."

DISCUSSION QUESTIONS

1. Can you think of a time when a disappointment focused your energy on a goal?

2. What is the downside of a single-minded purpose?

3. Do you have a problem with finishing things or quitting? Why or why not?

CHAPTER EIGHT
TRUSTWORTHY

SCRIPTURE—PSALM 111:7

"All he does is just and good, and all his commandments are trustworthy."

DISCUSSION QUESTIONS

1. What does being trustworthy mean today?

2. Do you have trouble trusting others? Why or why not?

3. Do you have trouble trusting God? Why or why not?

CHAPTER NINE
REJECTING PASSIVITY

SCRIPTURE—MARK 1:12-13

"Immediately, the Holy Spirit compelled Jesus to go into the wilderness. He was there for forty days, being tempted by Satan. He was out among the wild animals, and angels took care of him."

DISCUSSION QUESTIONS

1. Do you have difficulty confronting problems? What informs this response to problems?

2. Are you passive when it comes to resisting temptation? Think of an example.

3. Has there been a decision you regret when you "went along" on something?

CHAPTER TEN
ACCEPTING RESPONSIBILITY

SCRIPTURE—HEBREWS 5:5

"That is why Christ did not exalt himself to become High Priest. No, he was chosen by God, who said to him, 'You are my Son. Today I have become your Father.'"

DISCUSSION QUESTIONS

1. If you are a father, how did it feel the very first time you became one?

2. Did you want to make any changes in your spiritual life? Share about this.

3. Have you struggled at times in your life with accepting responsibility? Why do you think this is?

CHAPTER ELEVEN
GETTING CLEAN

SCRIPTURE—JAMES 4:7-8

*"So humble yourself before God. Resist the devil,
and he will flee from you. Draw close to God, and
God will draw close to you. Wash your hands, you
sinners; purify your hearts, you hypocrites."*

DISCUSSION QUESTIONS

1. How can a man wash his hands and purify his heart?

2. Do you look at other women even with your
   wife present? How does this make you feel?

3. What does it mean to have the mind of a mustang?

CHAPTER TWELVE
CHEERFUL

SCRIPTURE—PROVERBS 15:15

"For the poor, every day brings trouble; for the happy heart, life is a continual feast."

DISCUSSION QUESTIONS

1. What do you think this verse means by "continual feast"?

2. Do you have other male friendships who bring laughter into your life? If not, how might you begin to develop some?

3. Do you set aside time to play with others? Why or why not?

CHAPTER THIRTEEN
HELPFUL

SCRIPTURE—EPHESIANS 4:29

"Don't use foul or abusive language. Let everything you say be good and helpful, so that your words will be an encouragement to those who hear them."

DISCUSSION QUESTIONS

1. Do you help build others up according to their need? In what ways?

2. Share about a time when someone helped you when you really needed it?

3. Have you allowed unwholesome talk out of your mouth that was not helpful? Think about the situation and how you might have handled it differently.

CHAPTER FOURTEEN
COURTEOUS

SCRIPTURE—PROVERBS 18:22

*"The man who finds a wife finds a treasure
and receives favor from the Lord."*

DISCUSSION QUESTIONS

1. Why does a man who finds a wife
   receive favor from the Lord?

2. Why does the Bible refer to a wife as a treasure?

3. If you are married, are you treating your
   wife like a treasure? Why or why not?

CHAPTER FIFTEEN
KINDNESS

SCRIPTURE—GALATIANS 5:22

"But when the Holy Spirit controls our lives, he will produce this kind of fruit in us: love, joy, peace, patience, kindness, goodness, faithfulness, gentleness, and self-control. Here there is no conflict with the law."

DISCUSSION QUESTIONS

1. Can your friends and family see your fruit of the Spirit?

2. Is it easy or difficult for you to be kind to others? Why?

3. What is the best example you can recall when someone was kind to you?

CHAPTER SIXTEEN
INHERITANCE / GOD'S REWARD

SCRIPTURE—PSALMS 135:12

'He gave their land as an inheritance, a special possession to his people Israel."

DISCUSSION QUESTIONS

1. What have you inherited from your family of origin?

2. What would you like to leave as your inheritance to your family?

3. What do you think your children would like to receive from you as your legacy?

ABOUT THE AUTHOR

David L. Savage grew up as an Air Force brat in West Texas with a deep and rich scouting background beginning in Cub Scouts, achieving the rank of Eagle Scout, and earning the bronze, gold and silver palms, then establishing and leading a high adventure Explorer Post before heading to Texas A&M University to study engineering. The summer after graduating from Texas A&M, he worked as a backpacking guide, or Ranger, at Philmont Scout Ranch and Explorer Base in Cimarron, New Mexico.

He has a passion for history and geopolitics, which he has enriched through global job-related travel and extensive reading. He and his wife, Kimberly, have been married for eighteen years and live in Katy, Texas. They blended their families and raised four children, now grown.

He has written hundreds of poems and was the official Roaster-in-Chief at many company promotions and retirement events, all in verse. His rich sense of humor has been displayed as an amateur at the

Comedy Workshop in Houston and winning the Star Search contest in Chicago back in the late eighties. He also was the U.S. Regional Winner of the Tall Tales Contest for Toastmasters International in that same period.

Throughout his life, David has been involved with men's ministries from the Walk to Emmaus to Men's Fraternity, now known as Better Man, and taking two of his sons on a father-son retreat called "Christ in the Tetons." He considers his Alpha Tau Omega college fraternity "Brotherhood Award" one of his most cherished awards.

David has been a lifelong backpacker and outdoorsman and has been blessed to have a group of five older advisors who, along with David, call themselves "The Sixpack." They have backpacked for twenty-five years together to provide some of the rich and humorous stories he shares throughout his memoir, *The Savage Path*.

THESAVAGEPATH.COM